LEADERS OF THE SCIENTIFIC REVOLUTION™

JOHANNES KEPLER

DANIEL E. HARMON

Rosen YA™

New York

Published in 2018 by The Rosen Publishing Group, Inc.
29 East 21st Street, New York, NY 10010

First Edition

Library of Congress Cataloging-in-Publication Data

Names: Harmon, Daniel E., author.
Title: Johannes Kepler / Daniel E. Harmon.
Description: First edition. | New York, NY: Rosen Publishing, 2018. | Series: Leaders of the scientific revolution | Includes bibliographical references and index. | Audience: Grades 7–12.
Identifiers: LCCN 2017000143 | ISBN 9781508174721 (library bound)
Subjects: LCSH: Kepler, Johannes, 1571–1630—Juvenile literature. | Astronomers—Germany—Biography—Juvenile literature.
Classification: LCC QB36.K4 H35 2018 | DDC 520.92 [B] —dc23
LC record available at https://lccn.loc.gov/2017000143

Manufactured in China

CONTENTS

INTRODUCTION

Until the Scientific Revolution, practically all astronomers were observers, not theorists. That is, they collected data about the sun, moon, planets, and stars by observing the skies with the naked eye; primitive telescopes were not introduced until the early 1600s. A few were so bold as to suggest theories concerning the solar system. Developing theories, however, for the most part was left to philosophers.

Then came Johannes Kepler. The young German was studying to become a Lutheran clergyman when his interests began to focus on mathematics and astronomy. He methodically analyzed the information gathered by Nicolaus Copernicus, Galileo Galilei, Tycho Brahe, and other astronomers. Ultimately, he formulated a model of the solar system. Kepler proposed what came to be known as the laws of planetary motion (also called Kepler's laws).

The "revolutionaries" who effected the Scientific Revolution were not all of one mind. They learned from one another—and challenged one another's ideas. In astronomy, Copernicus, Galileo, Brahe, and Kepler came to varying levels of agreement. Fundamental arguments persisted, though, especially in the proposals of

Johannes Kepler clarified basic understandings of astronomers of his time. This portrait was made circa 1612, around the time he departed as court mathematician to Emperor Rudolf.

Copernicus and Brahe. Some of their differing theories were still tested long after the seventeenth century.

The prominent astronomer with whom Kepler worked closely was Brahe. An older man with decades of experience studying the planets, Brahe was Kepler's mentor for only a brief time. The experience was pivotal in young Kepler's career, however. Thanks to Brahe, Kepler became imperial mathematician to the Holy Roman emperor, a position that benefited him in many ways. Without that powerful credential, it's doubtful Kepler would have been able to gather the detailed evidence necessary to formulate his scientific principles or to have them published. Although Brahe drew erroneous conclusions, the data he gleaned from nightly stargazing would be vital to Kepler's later work.

At first, Kepler's theories won little respect. Within a century of his death in 1630, though, further observations of the planets and of solar and lunar eclipses proved he was correct on important points.

Although Kepler is best known for his planetary theories, he made other contributions to science as well. He suggested significant improvements to the telescope, which was just beginning to be used during his lifetime. Kepler made detailed studies of optics and explained what, exactly, makes it possible for people to see.

What may be most remarkable about the magnificent progress in knowledge made during the Scientific Revolution is that it was achieved during two centuries of social unrest across Europe. The Protestant break from the Roman Catholic Church resulted in years of unsettling discord and often violence. Kepler's own life was drastically affected by the turbulent political and religious climate. Even during his quarter century as the Holy Roman emperor's personal mathematician, he repeatedly was compelled to dodge persecution. Kepler felt constant opposition from Catholic authorities as well as from factions within the Protestant movement of which he was a member.

Like all great scientists, Kepler made mistakes. His lasting record, however, confirms him as one of the most important investigators and analysts of the Scientific Revolution. Much of the successful work of those who followed was made possible by Kepler's findings.

CHAPTER ONE

A Tumultuous Time for Science

Johannes Kepler (1571–1630) lived in the waning years of the European Renaissance. For three centuries, the continent had experienced steady advances in education, medicine, science, philosophy, the arts, and literature. Its societies had made significant changes during the Middle Ages and new kinds of political, social, cultural, and economic organizations appeared. These new forms became the foundations for the age of "enlightenment" and the modern period.

It was not, however, a time of peace and prosperity. Newly formed Christian sects broke away from the Roman Catholic Church, which had been the Christian religion of western Europe during the Middle Ages. This religious revolt, which separated the Christians

Violent religious unrest ravaged Europe during the sixteenth and seventeenth centuries. Here, Protestants attack a Catholic walled city in France.

into Protestants and Roman Catholics, was known as the Reformation. Religious conflicts during the Reformation often became violent and erupted across Europe with horrible consequences. Kings and princes used the religious upheaval in attempts to grasp new territories for themselves. It was a time of uncertainty.

THE WORLD IN KEPLER'S DAY

Without question, many important changes occured during the two centuries of the Scientific Revolution in Europe (from approximately 1500 to 1700). Remarkable discoveries brought about a fundamental rethinking of ideas. Subjects under scrutiny included the various sciences, religion, education, and exploration.

At the time of Johannes Kepler's birth, in the area of science, Nicolaus Copernicus (1473–1543) recently had turned the world on its ear with his radical theories of the solar system. In Italy, Galileo Galilei (1564–1642) was using his knowledge of physics and astronomy to invent a calculating compass and a primitive telescope. A young Danish nobleman named Tycho Brahe (1546–1601) was making remarkable observations of comets. Kepler saw one major comet, which appeared in 1577, when he was five years old at the time.

During the twenty years before and after Kepler's birth, explorers from European countries probed unknown lands around the world. Fledgling settlements were made in the Americas—the "New

The Great Comet of 1577, which Kepler observed with his mother from a hilltop, was so bright it sometimes could even be seen during the day.

World" across the Atlantic. Expeditions ventured into uncharted waters of the Atlantic, Pacific, and Indian Oceans. Soon, the East India companies of Denmark, the Netherlands, England, and France would be vying

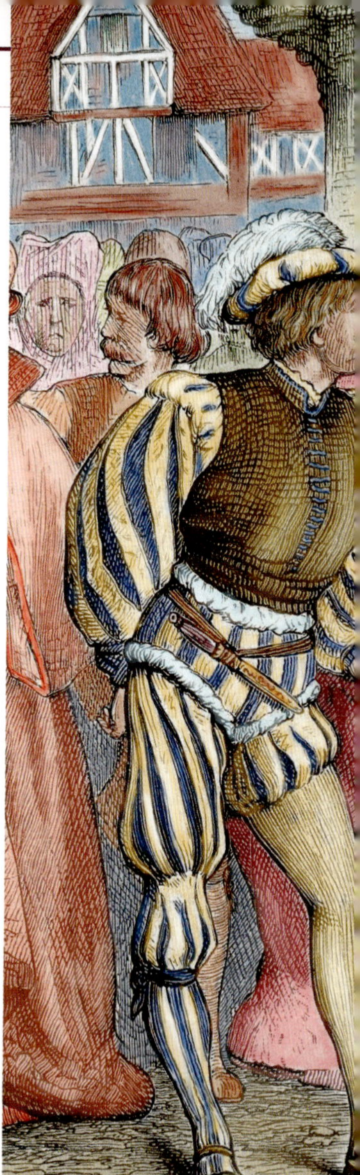

for control of trading rights with kingdoms in India and Asia.

In England, Elizabeth I (1533–1603) had recently been crowned queen. One of Kepler's contemporaries (whom he never met) was William Shakespeare (1564–1616).

It was an age of amazing inventions. A Swiss clockmaker named Joost Bürgi (1552–1632) in 1577 invented a clock with a minute hand. Three decades later, the first crude telescope was invented.

At the same time, power struggles were ongoing—not just among European princes, but between continents. To the east, in the year of Kepler's birth, Tartar invaders from what is now Turkey were attacking cities in southeastern Europe.

With all these developments, it also was a time of violent religious struggles across Europe. For centuries, the Roman Catholic Church, based in Rome, had been the dominant Christian religion throughout Europe. About fifty years before Johannes Kepler's birth, Martin Luther (1483–1546), a German Catholic monk and scholar, defied Catholic customs.

Martin Luther, in 1517, nailed his Ninety-Five Theses, points of opposition to Roman Catholic practices, to the door of the castle church in Wittenberg. The Protestant Revolution began.

Luther challenged the Catholic Church particularly for its longstanding practice of charging money for the forgiveness of sins. Luther proclaimed that everyone should have access to the Scriptures and everyone should be able to appeal directly to God for forgiveness, without paying money to the church. Luther's revolutionary teachings spread like wildfire. They began what is called the Protestant Reformation.

Many Christians, though, remained firmly loyal to the church leadership in Rome. Catholic popes had been the heads of the Christian faith for more than a millennium. To defy papal authority, devout Catholics believed, was sacrilegious.

The early decades of the Reformation were marred by bloody confrontations between steadfast Roman Catholics and Reformers. Reformers were primarily Lutherans in Germany, Huguenots in France, and Anglicans in England. Within a year of Kepler's birth, two incidents punctuated the turbulent state of affairs. In July 1572, Protestants executed nineteen Catholic priests in the Netherlands; the next month, Catholics slew and executed more than twenty thousand Huguenots throughout France.

BIRTH OF AN EMINENT SKY GAZER

Kepler was born on December 27, 1571, in Weil der Stadt. Weil der Stadt is a small, scenic town at the edge of the legendary Black Forest in what is now southwestern Germany. Established during the Middle Ages, it became a busy trading center. The town would be destroyed during the Thirty Years' War in 1648, after Kepler's death, but it quickly would be rebuilt. Many seventeenth-century structures still exist there. Tourists

The house where Kepler was born is shown on the main square of Weil der Stadt. The fountain statue is of seventeenth-century Emperor Charles V.

today are intrigued by its historic stone walls and towers. An annual carnival celebrates ancient German tribal traditions.

Several individuals of historical note were born in Weil der Stadt. They include Johannes Brenz (1499–1570), a leader of the Protestant Reformation in Germany. Kepler is the most famous person born there. Many citizens refer to their home as "Kepler City." His worldwide reputation as a leader of the Scientific Revolution has had a significant effect on the city's historic preservation. During World War II (1939–1945), French forces cancelled an artillery bombardment on Weil der Stadt when they realized it was Kepler's hometown.

Heinrich Kepler, the child's father, was a bully, a soldier of fortune, and a callous parent. When Johannes was born, the family members were living in the house of Heinrich's father, Sebaldus, who was mayor of Weil der Stadt. The Keplers had a noble heritage. In the previous century, an ancestor had been knighted by Sigismund (1368–1437), king of Hungary and Bohemia, for military gallantry. Later generations had declined in status, but Grandfather Sebaldus still was highly respected. Not so Heinrich, who went off to join an army in the Netherlands when Johannes, his first child, was three. Throughout Johannes's childhood, Heinrich repeatedly left home, returned, and left again. According to James R. Voelkel's book *Johannes Kepler and the New Astronomy*, the son later

A MARVEL IN THE NIGHT SKY

It came to be known as the Great Comet. It first appeared in November 1577 and was viewed nightly by people across Europe and Asia Minor for more than two months. The brilliant phenomenon, little understood then even by scientists, was stunning. Its tail was many times wider than a full moon.

Spellbound residents took to hilly summits away from city and village lights for a clearer view. One curious spectator was Katharina Kepler, whose family at the time was living in the village of Leonberg in southern Germany. She trudged up a nearby hill one evening with her oldest child, Johannes, to view the comet.

The boy, not yet six years old, apparently was not very impressed. It was cold, it was late, and his poor eyesight prevented him from fully appreciating the spectacle. Later in life, however, his study of calculations of the comet made by noted scientists of the day would help him formulate important theories about the solar system.

(*CONTINUED ON THE NEXT PAGE*)

(CONTINUED FROM THE PREVIOUS PAGE)

Throughout history, people have been superstitious about comets and have contrived amusing explanations for their appearances. Chinese observers in 240 BCE saw what now is named Halley's comet. They considered it a "broom star," swishing about the skies to clean up the cosmos. In pagan cultures, some believed comets were mighty weapons hurled against Earth by angry gods. Some held that when a comet was sighted, a king or queen would die. Even today, people in some cultures think comets are warnings of disasters.

would remember his father as a hot-tempered man who "destroyed everything."

His mother, Katharina, was the daughter of an innkeeper in Eltingen, a nearby village. She, like her husband, was argumentative and had few friends. The parents' relationship—when Heinrich was home—was predictably stormy.

Johannes was not a healthy child. He was small and had poor vision—a defect that, remarkably, did not substantially impair his work of observing the planets. But as history would prove, his physical deficiencies were more than compensated for by his intellect.

A NEW PLAYER ON THE STAGE OF DISCOVERERS

The arrival of Kepler onto the stage of scientific progress in the late sixteenth century was not only significant, it was unlikely. A sequence of unforeseeable events would bring him into contact with one of the leading astronomers of his day, Tycho Brah, and Kepler would become Brahe's assistant. Theirs was to be a rocky collaboration, but it would lead to crucial advances in astronomers' understanding of the solar system. Had it not been for that unexpected association, Kepler's life would have turned out very differently. Very probably, his name today would be unknown in world history.

The young Johannes Kepler could not have realized it as a child, but he was to play a major role in the Scientific Revolution. Throughout his life he would remain physically feeble. But in the end, he would become an intellectual giant.

CHAPTER TWO

Kepler Escapes to School

In his book *The Watershed: A Biography of Johannes Kepler*, historian Arthur Koestler described his subject as a man who "fought his way out" of a childhood that was "spent in hell." To say Johannes Kepler endured a difficult childhood would be a grave understatement. He was a puny youth, times were hard, and his parents failed to provide stable upbringings for their children. For Johannes, a great measure of relief came when, as a teenager, he went off to school. There, he was free from the household demands of his home life but would face new tests.

According to Kepler's personal genealogical account, which he wrote when he was twenty-six years old, he was born prematurely. He wrote of a crippling pain in his hands. His poor eyesight is believed to have been a combination of myopia (nearsightedness) and multiple vision. Young Johannes suffered from other disorders. A frail child, he had frequent stomach aches and often broke out in rashes and boils, which did not heal quickly. He was nervous, unable to sit still for very long.

WAYWARD PARENTS

His father, Heinrich, according to Johannes's record of the family, was unreliable at best as a parent. As a young man, Heinrich had learned gunnery and had become a soldier for hire. His father vainly hoped, Johannes believed, to win glory and nobility like their ancestor. This was not to be. In 1577, when Johannes was six years old, Heinrich committed a serious crime while away at war and narrowly escaped hanging, according to Johannes's personal records. Johannes did not state the crime involved. It was suggestive, though, of the troubled circumstances of his early years.

By that time, they were living in Leonberg, a village not far from Weil der Stadt. Their relocation apparently was prompted by the father's disgrace. He had

Heinrich Kepler, Johannes's father, frequently went off to fight as a mercenary soldier for one army or another. This watercolor depicts typical German soldiers of the sixteenth century.

joined a Catholic army to put down a Protestant revolt in the Netherlands, but Kepler family members in Weil der Stadt were staunch Protestants.

Heinrich repeatedly abandoned his family to go fight as a mercenary, returning home sooner or later.

During a prolonged stay at home, Heinrich opened a tavern, but this did not settle him down permanently. On one occasion, his wife, Katharina, went off to find him and bring him back from a military campaign, leaving the children in the care of their grandparents. Finally, in 1588, Heinrich went to war again—this time to serve as a naval captain. Historians believe he probably died in battle. He never returned. Johannes was just sixteen years old.

Kepler's mother was not as neglectful as his father, but she was fussy and eccentric. She created strange herbal concoctions and was said to have fashioned a drinking cup from her father's skull. Her weird behavior eventually would result in accusations that she was a witch.

When Heinrich was at home, the parents frequently quarreled. The household was in a constant state of tension. Johannes, for his part, found comfort in his Lutheran faith, in which he immersed himself from an early age. Biographer Max Caspar, in *Kepler*, explained, "In trials he sought the help of God, whom he revered as an omnipotent, all-governing and all-embracing power."

Because of their parents' instability, the children's education was sporadic. At age nine, Johannes was sent to labor on a farm for two years to help support the family. Because of his slight build and sickly health, it was a severe hardship. He also was hampered by the weakness of his hands, probably caused by an incident when

As a child, Kepler was forced to do farm labor, like the peasants shown in this vintage woodcut. Frail of stature, he was ill equipped for such toil.

he was three years old—after contracting smallpox, his grandmother bound severely tight to keep him from scratching the pox marks.

The prolonged period of farm work and his unsettled home life were setbacks to Kepler's early education. Latin studies elementary school ordinarily took three years to complete; it took Johannes six.

AN EDUCATION STEEPED IN LATIN

The Lutheran dukes of the Württemberg region of Germany understood the importance of education. A hallmark of Lutheranism was that all people should be able to read and interpret the Bible for themselves. The rulers established Protestant schools, many of them in former Catholic convents and monasteries. They employed Lutheran clergymen to teach.

Johannes Kepler's early learning took place first in a traditional German school, where students learned basic subjects including proper German. He then attended Latin schools. Latin was the dominant language taught—and often spoken—in European elementary schools and universities. It was considered the language of scholars. In advanced seminaries, Kepler also learned Greek and French.

His Latin education would markedly affect his profession. Most of the books and correspondence he wrote throughout his life were in Latin.

A BRILLIANT MIND EMERGES FROM DESPAIR

The child was an excellent student. He loved mental challenges and puzzles. He also enjoyed music and poetry, becoming something of a poet himself. His writings were complex and sometimes confusing as he moved from one thought to another, exploring a mixture of related ideas. To sharpen his mind, he memorized some of the longer Psalms from the Bible. He carefully considered everything he was taught, not necessarily taking the word of his teachers. Overall, he was one of the brightest students in the schools he attended.

He also applied his independent spirit and insistence on testing statements to ensure their accuracy to his religious education. In

The interior of a typical German schoolroom during Kepler's era is pictured here. For him, school was an escape from his troubled home life, and he excelled.

church, he did not take for granted everything that was preached. During the Reformation, Protestant theologians did not agree on every point. Discord was especially strong between German Lutherans and French Calvinists. When a preacher criticized the beliefs of another religious group, Kepler looked to the Bible to learn for himself what was written. At an early age, he developed a sense of tolerance for what others believed.

Happily for Kepler, the Württemberg duchy where he lived had excellent schools, seminaries, and universities. The Lutheran dukes found them useful for creating loyalty among the common folk. They established grants and scholarships for poor youths with promising intellects who completed the elementary and secondary schools. In return for room and board, students had to take an oath swearing lifelong allegiance to the duke. At thirteen, having decided to become a clergyman, Kepler made the pledge and was admitted to the seminary at Adelberg.

Latin was the language of the seminaries. Courses were taught in Latin, and students were urged to speak Latin in casual conversation. The courses taught during Kepler's two years at Adelberg, followed by two years at the seminary in Maulbronn, included theology, classical literature, mathematics, philosophy, Greek, French, and music. Kepler also studied dialectics and rhetoric—which today might be defined as "communication skills."

This aerial view depicts the walled monastery at Maulbronn, where Kepler completed his lower seminary studies. He was rewarded for his achievements with a scholarship to the University of Tübingen.

Daily life for seminary students was severe. In winter, they began classes at five o'clock in the morning, in summer at four o'clock. Students rarely were allowed to go home on visits.

For Kepler, an added hardship was his unpopularity. He seems to have made many more enemies than friends among his classmates. Part of the reason was his superior intellect and high class rankings. It also no doubt stemmed from his aggressively competitive nature. He often got into fights and, because of his frailness, usually lost. He kept a record of schoolmates he considered his enemies, with notes about the reasons he disliked them.

In his autobiographical records, Kepler noted what seem to be contradictions about himself during this stage of his life. For example, he hated to waste time but confessed that he caught himself wasting it constantly. His appearance, he wrote, was like that of a "little lap dog." He did not enjoy conversation, and he always greeted people meekly, "just like a little dog." He had simple wants and needs. Kepler wrote that he depended heavily on others, apparently lacking confidence in himself. He imitated other students and constantly tried to stay on friendly terms. Yet, he wrote that when he felt mistreated, he would "growl" and "bark" at the offender. His "barks" took the form of sharp criticisms and often led to fights.

He also described himself as daringly reckless. He no doubt inherited this trait from his wandering, warring father. Johannes, though, believed the cause of his wild streak was the alignment of the planets and moon. The link between human nature and celestial objects, to him, would become an essential assumption in his future astronomical studies.

PREPARING FOR THE CLERGY

Kepler completed his studies at the medieval seminary in Maulbronn in September 1588. The following year, the duke of Württemberg awarded him and four other students scholarships to the higher seminary at the University of Tübingen. There, he planned to undergo five years of advanced study that would lead to a life as a Lutheran minister.

Kepler threw himself into this stage of his education. As before, his intellect and diligence kept him at the head of his class. The result, though, was to be quite different from what he imagined. He was destined to become not a preacher but a teacher. The church would lose a brilliant theologian. Science would gain a brilliant mathematical mind.

CHAPTER THREE

The Student Becomes a Scholar

Tübingen lies along the heights where the Ammer and Steinlach Rivers flow into the Neckar. For centuries, Tübingen has been essentially a university town. Today, a third of its population is comprised of students. It also has a history as a center for celestial studies. An astronomical clock constructed in 1511 still adorns the façade of the town hall. Farmers for centuries used it to signal when to plant and gather their crops. It tracked the time, moon phases, seasons, and other data.

The city is about 55 miles (89 kilometers) south of the Maulbronn monastery. Historians believe Kepler may have made the journey there on foot along the forest byways.

This is the ornately-painted façade of the Rathaus, or city hall, in Tübingen. The astronomical clock at the roof, built almost a century before Kepler lived, is a noted tourist attraction.

SCRUTINIZING COPERNICUS

At the Tübingen seminary, Kepler began to analyze carefully an important theory proposed by Nicolaus Copernicus in 1543. The Polish scientist had stated that the solar system is heliocentric. This declaration meant the sun is at the center of our solar system and the planets orbit around it. This understanding of the universe was radically new. For 1,500 years, astronomers had embraced the theory of second-century mathematician Claudius Ptolemaeus (Ptolemy), who assumed Earth is at the center. Ptolemy's Earth-centered model is termed "geocentric."

Copernicus also taught that Earth rotates from west to east on a north-south axis; one day on earth represents one complete rotation. These theories of heliocentricity and earthly rotation form what became known as the Copernican system of astronomical thought.

The eager young seminarian was greatly influenced by Michael Maestlin, his professor of mathematics and astronomy. Maestlin (1550–1631) was a former Lutheran minister; he also was a knowledgeable astronomer. At the time Kepler entered seminary, most astronomers had not yet accepted Copernicus's proposals. They reckoned that if Earth was spinning and zooming rapidly through space, people would feel the motions and animals and objects would fly off the surface of the planet. Ironically, Maestlin still taught Ptolemy's

The dramatic theories of astronomer Nicolaus Copernicus were not widely accepted by contemporary scientists. Kepler, however, became convinced that Copernicus fundamentally was right.

system of astronomy to his students—but he had come to believe Copernicus was right. He let Kepler borrow his copy of *De Revolutionibus Orbium Coelestium* (*On the Revolutions of the Heavenly Spheres*), published by Copernicus in 1543. Maestlin explained to him details of Copernicus's teachings that seemed unclear.

To young Kepler, who was devoutly religious, Copernicus's heliocentric theory made sense. It agreed perfectly with his theological understanding. He saw the universe as the perfect design of God. It appeared obvious to him that the all-powerful sun would be at the center—God the Father. The second part of the holy Trinity, Jesus the Son, was represented by the outer extremities of the solar system. The third part, the Holy Spirit, was the space between the center and the circumference.

Even at this early stage of his scientific investigations, Kepler's inborne curiosity was honest and objective. He did not aggressively set out to prove a point of view without examining it from all sides. According to historian Kitty Ferguson, in her book *Tycho & Kepler*, Kepler once said of his early work, "There was nothing I could state that I could not also contradict."

Despite his chronic health issues and study disciplines, Kepler's teen years and young adulthood were not without pleasures. His diary tells of his excitement acting in a carnival play. He also indulged in a bit of gambling—though not profitably.

In Europe during Kepler's time, fireworks exhibits provided popular entertainment for commoners as well as the aristocracy. The festival pictured here took place at Stuttgart, Germany, in 1616.

EARLY END TO KEPLER'S EDUCATION

Kepler received another university degree in 1591 after finishing the first phase of his clerical studies. His professors were delighted with his progress and his exceptional level of intelligence. He entered a higher level of his scholarship, a three-year program of applied theological training.

What happened next was completely unexpected. A small Protestant seminary in the city of Graz, capital of the province of Styria in Austria, was in need of a mathematics teacher. It asked the faculty at the Tübingen seminary to send one of their finest students to fill the position.

Kepler was looking forward to finishing his seminary studies and entering the clergy. When his mentors recommended him to go to Graz, he was torn. Graz was almost 300 miles (483 km) to the east, a grueling, month-long, overland journey from his home region. He would be far away from everyone he knew. Furthermore, the prospect of teaching mathematics at a small school did not appeal to him. He felt that his real calling was church service.

However, he sensed that there must be a need at the Graz seminary. It would be a situation in which he might be able to serve in a different way. After anguished soul-searching, he accepted the request. In March 1594, he left Tübingen, where he had learned and assessed so much about the theories of the universe. He determined to become a humble schoolteacher.

Some historians speculate that the Tübingen seminary leaders sent Kepler packing off to Graz because of his nonconformist views as a leading student. He had debated in defense of Copernicus's astronomical theories, which still had not been widely accepted. Worse, he sympathized with Calvinists, whom many German Lutherans despised.

Whatever their reasons for recommending him, and whatever his reasons for going, away he went. Kepler was to spend the next six years teaching math while groping more deeply into the realities of the universe.

SLOW RISE TO RECOGNITION

Kepler's reception at Graz was a bit unnerving. The school administrators were welcoming. Students, however, found him boring—not surprisingly, because Kepler felt inadequate as a young teacher. Their uncomplimentary first impression was spread throughout the school. Few students attended his class the first year. The next year, he had no students. He wrote a letter to Maestlin, his old tutor of math and astronomy at Tübingen. Could the professor find him any sort of teaching role back in his homeland?

But there were no prospects for a return. Surprisingly, meanwhile, his employers seemed unconcerned

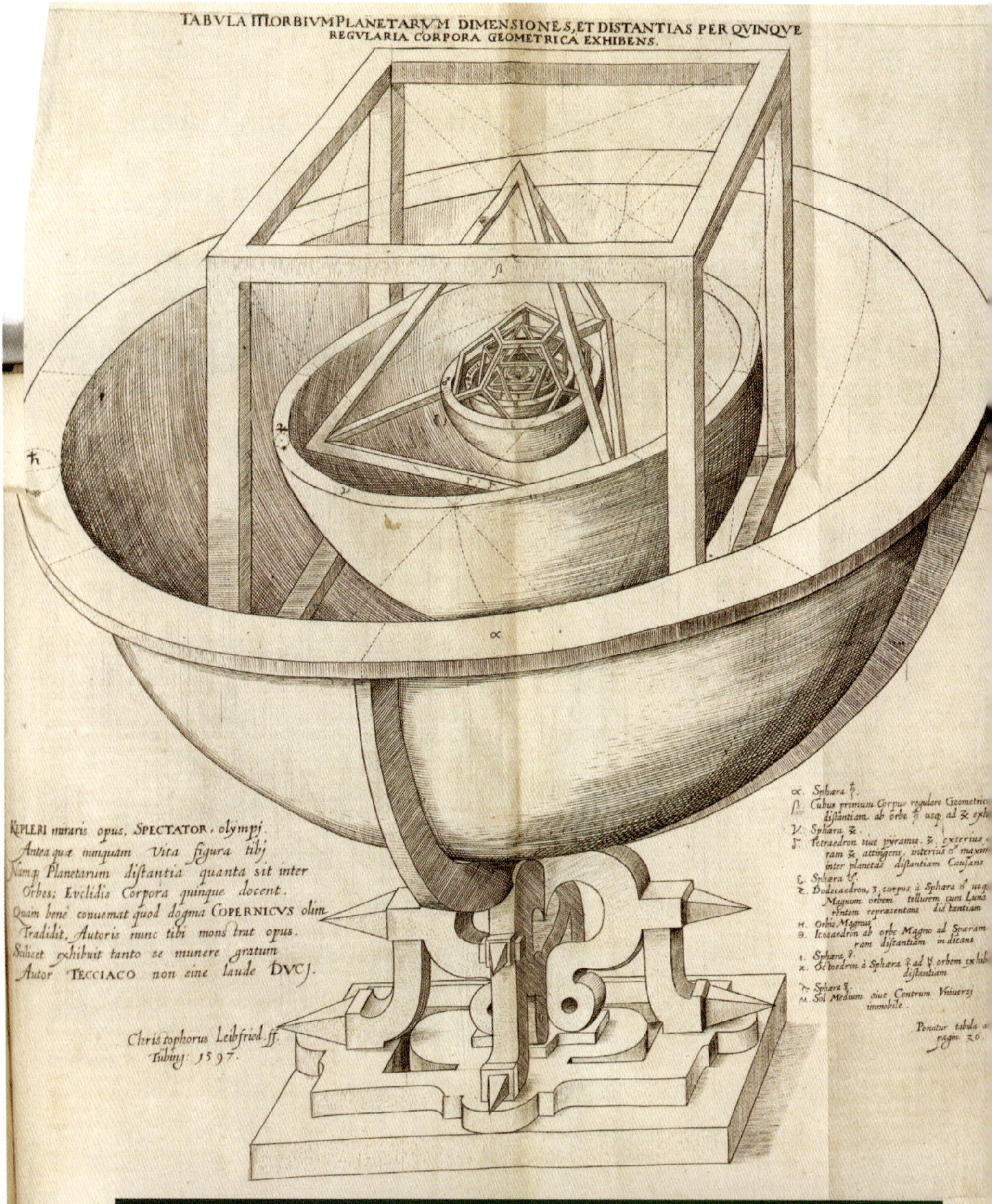

This illustration depicting Kepler's model of the universe was published in *Mysterium Cosmographicum*. Different spheres represent the orbits of planets; the outer sphere is that of Saturn.

about his students lack of enthusiasm. Mathematics, they pointed out reassuringly, was not a particularly popular subject among students. They liked him and respected his intellectual capabilities.

By all accounts, Kepler was not an inspiring teacher at Graz. He may have learned more from his Graz experience than the students did. One day in July 1595, a diagram he was drawing on a blackboard suddenly stopped him in his thoughts. It occurred to him that the universe consists of symmetrical configurations (cubes, triangles, and so forth). He elaborated on the concept in *Mysterium Cosmographicum* (Cosmographic Mystery), his first book, which was published the next year.

Mysterium Cosmographicum (later translated into English as *The Secret of the Universe*) was neither a scholarly nor financial success for the fledgling astronomer. It had little chance. During those decades of the Scientific Revolution, books about science were published in Germany at a rate of more than a thousand each year. Kepler had to buy two hundred copies himself, paying cash, to cover the printing cost. He sent copies of the little book to leading scientists across Europe, including Galileo. Some took notice, but the reception was less than enthusiastic. An added insult came at the book fair in Frankfurt, where he hoped to sell copies and gain recognition. His last name was misspelled in the program as "Repleus."

MARRIAGE TO A MILLER'S DAUGHTER

Several of Kepler's friends in Graz were inclined to be matchmakers. They believed they had found the perfect wife for the young mathematician. His courtship of Barbara Mühleck (also known as Müller), daughter of a local miller, was a comedy of refusals and missteps, but with a satisfactory result.

Barbara was only twenty-three years old but had already been married twice. Both husbands had died. Her father was wealthy. He was not at all impressed by the lowly, ill-paid schoolteacher. At first, he refused Kepler's proposal. Pressed by Kepler's friends over a period of months, he agreed. Kepler was away on a trip at that time, though. By the time he returned, the cautious miller had withdrawn his consent. Kepler's colleagues renewed their efforts, recruiting church officials and the seminary dean to speak to the miller in support of their friend. The father relented once more. Johannes and Barbara were married on April 27, 1597.

Kepler was devoted to his bride, but not altogether content. He described her in his family records as "simple of mind and fat of body." He was dismayed to realize that his life again had taken a dramatic and unexpected turn. "Thus, with one blow," he recorded, "all my plans for beginning another life collapsed."

The idea Kepler proposed in *Mysterium Cosmographicum* eventually proved to be incorrect. Still, it was a springboard for what would come to be known as Kepler's laws.

ASTRONOMY VERSUS ASTROLOGY

Among Kepler's duties while at Graz was that we would find curious today: compiling a yearly astrological calendar. Astrology today is considered a superstition or, at best, a parascience. It is given little or no credence by modern scholars. Astrologers consider events that happen on Earth to be results of celestial activities. For example, astrologers believe an individual's personal characteristics, daily happenings, and ultimate future are determined by the locations of the sun, moon, planets, and stars at the moment of birth. Even today, millions of people around the world check their astrological horoscopes every morning. They believe astrology can give them guidance about all facets of their lives, including marriage and careers. Astrologers also predict world events based on celestial changes. Scientists scoff.

In Kepler's day, astrology was deemed a field of science. Many of the early astronomers were also dedicated astrologers. So was Kepler, at least to some extent. It is significant that at the end of his life, he was serving as the official astrologer for Albrecht Wenzel Eusebius von Wallenstein, a powerful Bohemian

Albrecht Wenzel Eusebius von Wallenstein engaged Kepler to be his official astrologer—a pseudoscience that Kepler once ridiculed as "monkey's play."

general who attempted to unite Germany during the Thirty Years' War. In parts of Kepler's writings, he appeared to take a serious interest in the possibilities of astrology. However, Koestler pointed out that over the years Kepler referred to astrology as "monkey play" and a "stepdaughter of astronomy."

Whatever his convictions about it, Kepler seemed to enjoy his assignment as the Graz seminary's astrologer. And he appeared to be good at it. The first calendar he assembled predicted a lethally frigid winter and an invasion of Austria by a Turkish army. Both prophesies came true.

FORCED RELOCATION

Graz in the 1590s was a center of opposition to the Protestant Reformation. Besides tension between Protestants and Catholics, there was disagreement among Protestants. Notably, many German Lutherans did not respect the beliefs of Calvinists, members of a Protestant movement that had begun in France. Kepler himself believed Lutherans and Calvinists were equal Christians. This view alienated him from some of his fellow Lutherans.

Kepler found himself in growing jeopardy at Graz. In 1598, a number of Protestant clergymen and educators were expelled from the city. Kepler was allowed to remain. Anti-Protestant leaders respected his knowledge as a mathematician and as an astrologer.

Yet, Kepler suspected his time in Graz was drawing to an unpleasant end.

He was concerned not just for his own well-being. In 1597, he had married Barbara Mühleck, daughter of a prominent miller in Graz. They were starting a family, although their first two children died in infancy.

He was rescued from his looming crisis in January 1600. Johann Friedrich Hoffmann was a nobleman who shared Kepler's fascination with astronomy and admired his exceptional intelligence. Importantly, Hoffmann was an adviser to Rudolf II, the Holy Roman emperor whose court was at Prague in Bohemia.

In that month, Hoffmann set out from Graz in his carriage, bound for the imperial court to the north. He invited Kepler to join him and to meet the emperor's official mathematician, noted astronomer and nobleman Tycho Brahe. It was a journey that marked what was no doubt the most critical turning point in Johannes Kepler's life.

CHAPTER FOUR

A Momentous Collaboration

Kepler found a satisfactory welcome at Prague, although the first year would turn out to be somewhat insecure. Tycho Brahe had read some of Kepler's writings. He invited Kepler to join his staff of assistants.

The two men were different in most ways. Brahe was from an upper-class upbringing; Kepler was a commoner. Brahe had almost forty years of experience observing the skies and had written twenty volumes of notations; Kepler was virtually unknown among scientists. Brahe was overbearing and argumentative, Kepler much more withdrawn. Nevertheless, they complemented each other's work very well.

Tycho Brahe, who became Kepler's mentor, was one of the foremost astronomers and instrument makers of the period. He also was a wealthy nobleman.

Their brief collaboration would have a great impact on the body of knowledge that emerged from the Scientific Revolution.

TYCHO BRAHE: BRILLIANT AND BLUSTERY

Tycho Brahe was a brilliant mathematician and one of the most important astronomers of the sixteenth century—although prone to error. He was only a teenager in 1560 when he witnessed a partial eclipse of the sun. This event may have inspired him to commit himself to a lifelong study of celestial objects and phenomena.

Brahe was born in Knudstrup, in the Scania region of Denmark (Scania became part of Sweden in 1658), to a wealthy family. He grew to become a nobleman as well as a scientist. Ferguson, in *Tycho & Kepler*, referred to Brahe as "a prince among astronomers and an astronomer among princes." He began his nightly studies of the skies while in his teens, equipped with only a globe and two compasses. Still, he was able to identify mistakes in the published astronomical tables. Brahe set about in earnest to correct them, making extensive notes.

The young scientist's inherited fortune enabled him to begin acquiring the finest astronomical instruments of his time. He built an impressive observatory at Hven (also known as Ven), an island in Øresund Sound, a waterway between Denmark and Sweden. He learned from the records of Ptolemy and Copernicus but did not embrace the ideas of either of his predecessors. He formed his own theories of the positions of stars and motions of planets.

Brahe had a tempestuous reputation. When he was a young man, he got into a sword duel over a mathematical argument. His nose was severed in the fight, and he lived the rest of his life with a prosthetic nose made of a flesh-colored metal composite.

Solar and lunar eclipses were of obvious interest to Brahe and other cosmologists. While living at Hven, he witnessed two total eclipses of the moon in 1577. This was also the year of the Great Comet, which Kepler viewed as a child. Brahe took thousands of careful measurements of the comet's path and size. He drew sketches and made detailed notes about the comet over a span of seventy-four nights in late 1577 and early 1578. This material became the substance of his book about the comet, published a decade later. Although Brahe erroneously assumed Earth was the center of the

A seventeenth-century print shows Tycho Brahe's elaborate island observatory at Hven as it looked in 1584. Most of the facility was underground. A rotating canopy housed a variety of instruments.

solar system, he was correct in theorizing that comets are physical objects traveling in space. This notion contradicted Galileo, who believed they were simply optical displays.

In the years just before his association with Kepler, Brahe had weathered a sequence of setbacks. His benefactor, King Frederick II of Denmark, died in 1588. King Christian IV, the successor, was not interested in Brahe's work. Brahe lost his financial backing and, later, his observatory at Hven. To his relief, Rudolf II, the Holy Roman emperor, invited him to come under his wing at Prague in 1597. Rudolf gave him a generous salary and a castle outside the city. Soon, a new observatory was under construction there, although Brahe would not live to see it completed. He was able to keep a staff of instrument makers, apprentices, and scholars to assist him.

BRAHE AND KEPLER

It is hardly surprising that the relationship between Kepler and Brahe was often stormy. This tension was not simply because of Brahe's arrogance and fiery temperament. A major point of contention was their difference of opinion about the theories of Nicolaus Copernicus. Kepler respected Copernicus's ideas, but Brahe never brought himself to accept entirely their predecessor's new order of the solar system.

At that time, five other planets had been detected. Brahe was willing to agree that those planets revolved around the sun. He decided, though, that they all—planets and sun—orbited Earth, which he insisted did not move.

Even before they met, Kepler, in his writings, had made contemptuous comments about the famous, lavishly equipped astronomer at Prague. Koestler cited one particular insult: "He is superlatively rich," Kepler sneered, "but he knows not how to make proper use of it, as is the case with most rich people."

Kepler was not especially happy with the tasks Brahe assigned him. He hoped to obtain access to the wealth of data Brahe had collected about the planets to help prove his own early hypothesis, described in *Mysterium Cosmographicum*. Brahe, he found to his disappointment, was unwilling to share his notes. Kepler would benefit, though, from one task he was given: helping make observations of Mars. This knowledge would be valuable in proving his first important law—that Mars and the other planets orbit the sun elliptically, not in perfect circles.

Despite their sometimes strained relationship, Brahe ensured Kepler's well-being. For a time in 1600, Kepler's employment with Brahe was not guaranteed, and he had not been completely released from his post in Graz. After months of uncertainty, Brahe assured him that his place with him in Prague was secure. In 1601,

A SCIENCE-MINDED RULER

Rudolf II (1552–1612) was not just the king of Bohemia (now the Czech Republic) and Hungary during the first half of Johannes Kepler's life. Rudolf was the Holy Roman emperor. The Holy Roman Empire extended across central Europe and included areas of France. Imperial mathematician in Rudolf's court was no minor role.

Historians believe Rudolf evidenced signs of insanity, but there is no doubt about his great passion in life: science. A collector of odd instruments and objects, Rudolf, in 1597, welcomed to his court in Prague the intriguing astronomer from Denmark, Tycho Brahe. Brahe was gifted with not only great intellect but also courtly charm. Brahe brought with him a massive library of three thousand books and an assortment of curious scientific instruments.

Rudolf was captivated by his Danish friend. He made Brahe his court mathematician—an appointment that soon would pass on to Johannes Kepler.

Rudolf II was Holy Roman emperor and king of Bohemia. A devotee of science, he appointed Kepler to be his imperial mathematician.

Kepler's situation was strengthened. Many of Brahe's other assistants left or died, leaving Kepler as his most reliable and knowledgeable colleague.

The association between Brahe and Kepler was short-lived. Brahe died on October 24, 1601. At the time, people believed he had lapsed into a fatal stupor after a banquet at which he drank excessively. Modern scientists, who exhumed his remains in 2010, determined that he most likely died from mercury poisoning. Historians can only speculate whether he was murdered or poisoned accidentally.

On his deathbed, Brahe begged Kepler not to promote Copernicus's model of the solar system. Historians report his famous, poignant last statement, which he moaned repeatedly: "Let me not seem to have lived in vain." How Kepler responded at bedside, if he said anything at all, is not known. Regardless, he soon began using Brahe's research to confirm in his own mind that Copernicus was right.

Brahe was given a grand funeral in Prague on November 4. Two days later, Kepler was appointed imperial mathematician.

THE EMPEROR'S MATHEMATICIAN

After Brahe's death, as the new imperial mathematician, Kepler was assigned to finish the books Brahe had been working on. He also acquired the mathematical instruments and notes that Brahe had compiled during his many years of study. Examples of Brahe's unique instruments included a trigonal (triangular) sextant and an equatorial armillary sphere. A sextant is used to measure the angle between two distant objects—Earth's horizon and a star, for example. Brahe's armillary sphere was a globe-like contraption used to pinpoint the positions of stars. Brahe described and sketched a number of instruments in his book *Astronomiae Instauratae Mechanica* (1598; Instruments for the Restoration of Astronomy).

Tycho Brahe accumulated and made an impressive collection of valuable scientific instruments, few of which existed at the time. Pictured here is his astronomical sextant.

In earnest, Kepler set about trying to fully understand the planets' orbits around the sun. Like Copernicus before him, he at first believed the orbits were circular. Kepler labored in frustration for eight years. In the end, he would come to realize their orbits must not be circles, but ellipses. This insight changed his mathematical approach to calculating planetary motion.

Kepler's position as imperial mathematician was disputed by Franz Tengnagel, a nobleman who was Brahe's son-in-law. Tengnagel, jealous that Kepler had been given charge of Brahe's research and tools, persuaded Emperor Rudolf that Kepler was lazy. As a result, Rudolf transferred to Tengnagel the authority to continue work on the important—and lucrative—project that Brahe had begun. The *Tabulae Rudolphinae* was an exhaustive collection of astronomical tables. Such tables precisely calculate the positions of planets in relation to known stars on a given date. They could be used, for example, to locate the planets and identify stars in the night sky. Tengnagel was paid very well to continue the work of his father-in-law—twice the salary that Kepler received from the imperial treasury. Tengnagel later would abandon the project, which Kepler would finish.

With this setback, Kepler turned his attention to two of his own books. The *Ad Vitellionem Paralipomena, Quibus Astronomiae Pars Optica Traditur* (also known as *Astronomiae Pars Optica* [1604; Supplement to Witelo (Latin: Vitellio), in Which Is Expounded the Optical Part of Astronomy]; published in English as *Optics: Paralipomena to Witelo, and Optical Part of Astronomy*) was based on an essay he had written in 1600 (Witelo was a thirteenth-century Polish scientist who wrote a book on optics that became the standard reference on the subject until the seventeenth century). It dealt with the use of pinhole images to study solar eclipses. Brahe had made a pinhole through which sunlight passed onto a white surface during a partial eclipse. Brahe had concluded, incorrectly, that it was impossible for the moon to fully block out the view of the sun from Earth during an eclipse. Kepler theorized that the size of the pinhole was an important variable and was the cause of Brahe's mistake.

His other book began as a study of the motion of Mars. It would grow to become his landmark contribution to science, *Astronomia Nova* (*New Astronomy*).

Ultimately, Tycho Brahe's observations and detailed notes and measurements provided much of the basis for Kepler's findings. They were central to Kepler's development of his laws of planetary motion.

CHAPTER FIVE

COPERNICUS'S CHAMPION

Johannes Kepler's classic work, *Astronomia Nova*, was years in the making. He began work on it in 1602; it wasn't published until 1609. It explained the two major laws of planetary science that he had formulated: that the orbits of the planets around the sun are elliptical (oval), not circular; and that a planet's orbit spans the same area of space, or "sweep," in every orbit (dubbed the "area law" by astronomers).

A pioneering point of his theories was that the motions of planets could be fully understood only by understanding the physical cause of their motions. Kepler's concept of planetary physics would prove to be in error. His ideas, though, profoundly influenced the thinking of astronomers and other scientists who followed after him. They played a role, for example, in

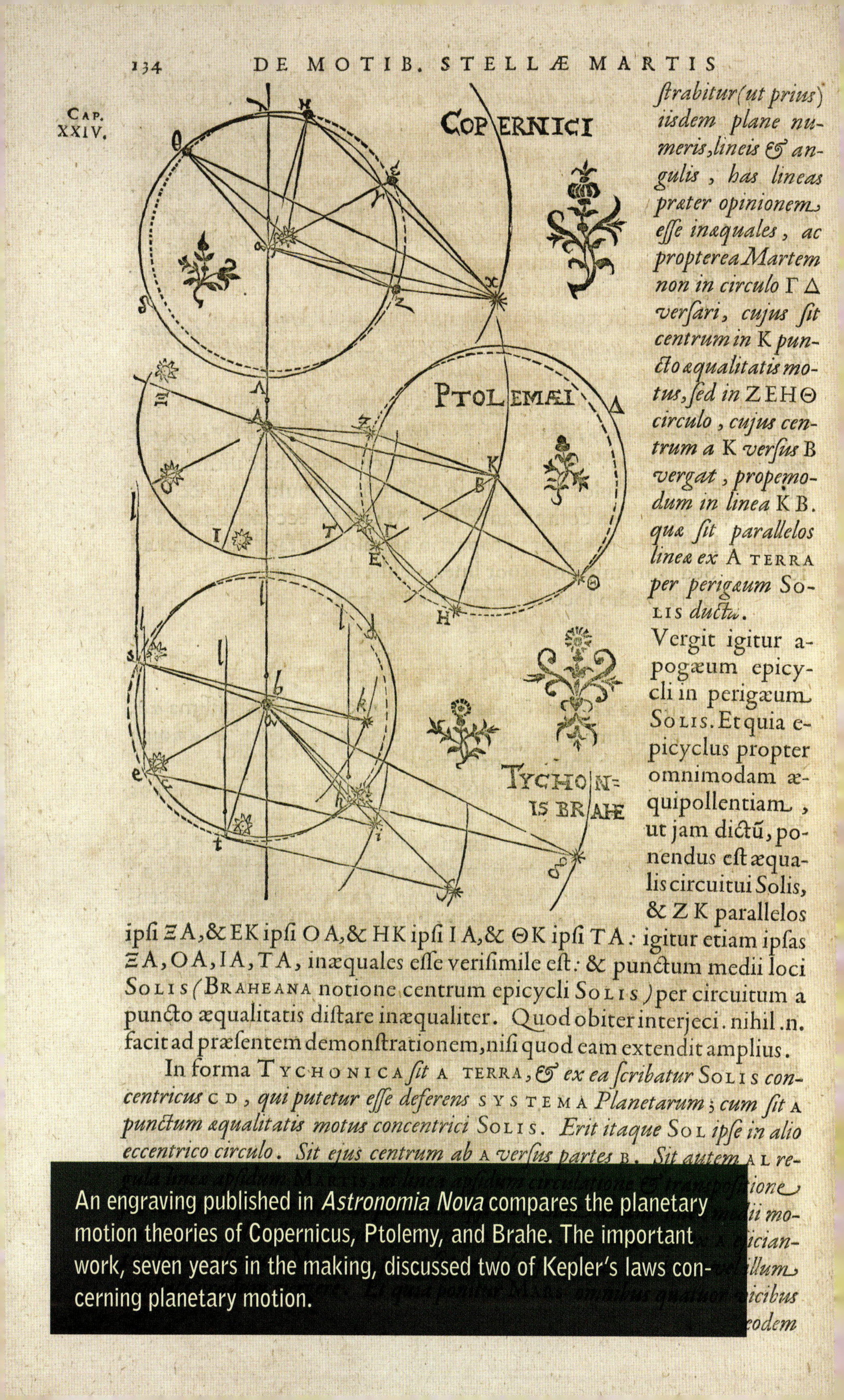

134 DE MOTIB. STELLÆ MARTIS

CAP. XXIV.

strabitur (ut prius) iisdem plane numeris, lineis & angulis, has lineas præter opinionem esse inæquales, ac propterea Martem non in circulo Γ Δ versari, cujus sit centrum in K *puncto æqualitatis motus, sed in* ZEHΘ *circulo, cujus centrum a* K *versus* B *vergat, propemodum in linea* KB. *quæ sit parallelos lineæ ex* A TERRA *per perigæum* SOLIS *ducta.*

Vergit igitur apogæum epicycli in perigæum SOLIS. Et quia epicyclus propter omnimodam æquipollentiam, ut jam dictũ, ponendus est æqualis circuitui Solis, & Z K parallelos ipsi ΞA, & EK ipsi OA, & HK ipsi IA, & ΘK ipsi TA: igitur etiam ipsas ΞA, OA, IA, TA, inæquales esse verisimile est: & punctum medii loci SOLIS (BRAHEANA notione centrum epicycli SOLIS) per circuitum a puncto æqualitatis distare inæqualiter. Quod obiter interjeci. nihil .n. facit ad præsentem demonstrationem, nisi quod eam extendit amplius.

In forma TYCHONICA *sit* A TERRA, *& ex ea scribatur* SOLIS *concentricus* CD, *qui putetur esse deferens* SYSTEMA *Planetarum; cum sit* A *punctum æqualitatis motus concentrici* SOLIS. *Erit itaque* SOL *ipse in alio eccentrico circulo. Sit ejus centrum ab* A *versus partes* B. *Sit autem* AL *re-*

... *ione* ... *ii mo-* ... *cian-* ... *illum* ... *vicibus* ... *eodem*

An engraving published in *Astronomia Nova* compares the planetary motion theories of Copernicus, Ptolemy, and Brahe. The important work, seven years in the making, discussed two of Kepler's laws concerning planetary motion.

the concept of gravity described by Sir Isaac Newton (1642–1727).

Astronomia Nova had been in print only a few months when news of a fantastic discovery overshadowed it. Galileo Galilei, it was reported, had identified four new planets. As it turned out, Galileo had found four large moons of Jupiter, not planets. Galileo published his discoveries in a small book titled *Sidereus Nuncius* (*The Sidereal Messenger* or *The Starry Messenger*).

The incident served to introduce Kepler into the elite circle of European astronomers. Kepler was, after all, the Holy Roman emperor's newly appointed mathematician. Galileo sent him a copy of the book and asked his opinion of it. Kepler could only generalize. Galileo had been making new discoveries of the heavens with his primitive telescopes; Kepler had no telescope available to confirm Galileo's observations. Nonetheless, he announced that he was confident Galileo's findings were correct.

Not everyone at the time of its publication was impressed by Kepler's *Astronomia Nova*. His most notable

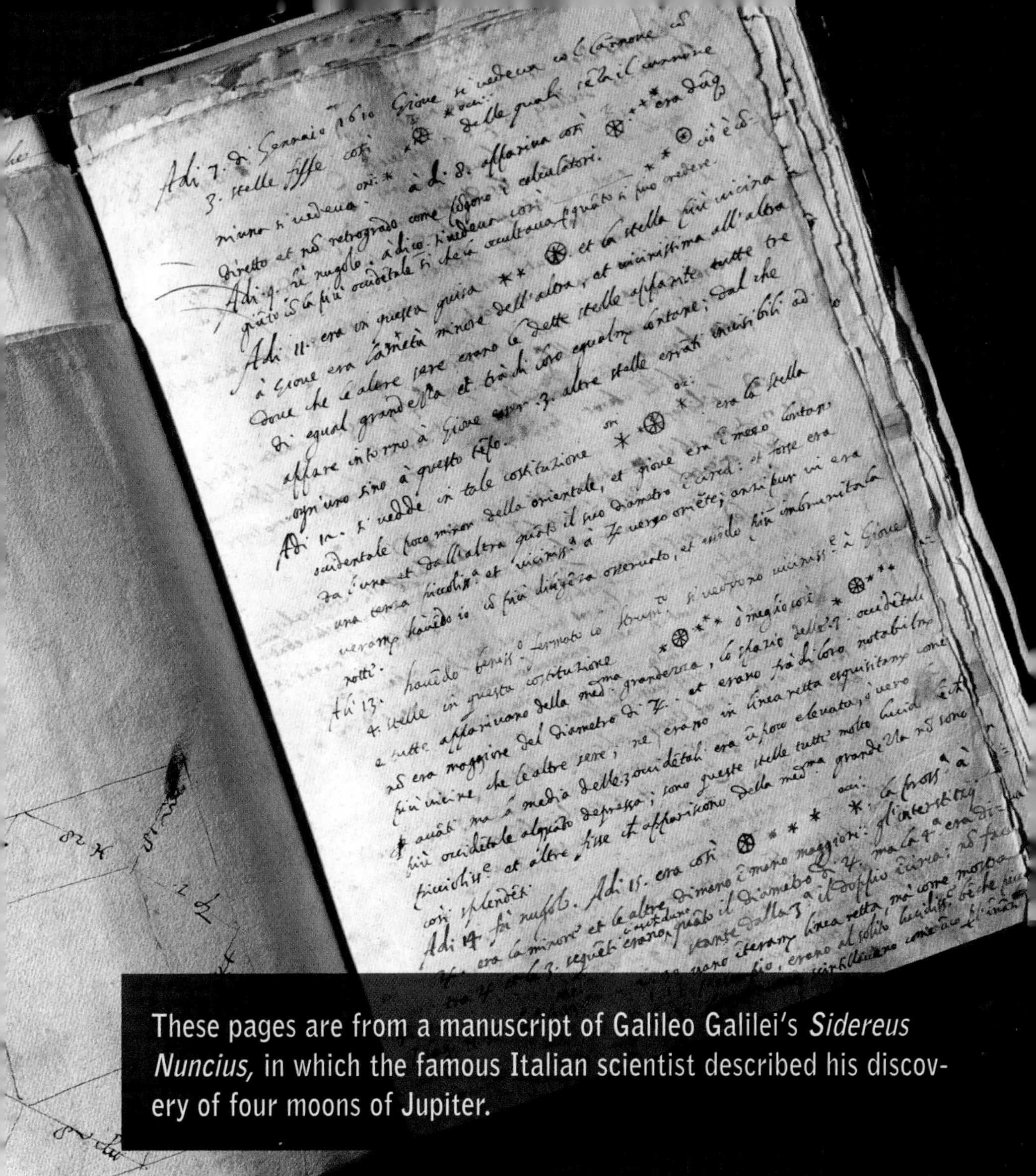

These pages are from a manuscript of Galileo Galilei's *Sidereus Nuncius,* in which the famous Italian scientist described his discovery of four moons of Jupiter.

critic was Franz Tengnagel. Kepler had agreed to let Brahe's son-in-law review the book before it was published. The men had been at odds ever since Brahe's death, and Tengnagel was scathing in his opinion of Kepler's finished work. The root of his anger was Kepler's support of Copernicus's ideas, which differed from Brahe's. Even despite Brahe's deathbed plea, Kepler did not shift his ground. He knew Copernicus was right.

Tengnagel obtained the right to pen a preface to the book. In it, he attacked Kepler for disagreeing with Brahe. He warned readers not to be influenced by Kepler's theories.

His enemy's criticism had little effect on Kepler's well-deserved reputation. By the time *Astronomia Nova* was published, the once-struggling mathematics teacher of Graz had risen to scientific fame throughout Europe and in England. His patron, Emperor Rudolf, publicly showered him with praise. However, Rudolf was stingy with financial support. The emperor took most of the profits from Kepler's books. Although he announced handsome salary increases for his court mathematician, Rudolf was slow in delivering the money. A large portion of it was never paid.

Kepler's relationship with the emperor was complicated by Rudolf's mental state. Rudolf had become a virtual hermit and rarely was seen outside the royal chambers. Many believed he was going insane. His royal family secretly planned to have his younger brother Matthias replace him as Holy Roman emperor. Matthias raised an army against him in 1608. Rudolf was intimidated. Without a struggle, he agreed to give his brother control of Hungary and two smaller domains, although for the time being, he remained the king of Bohemia.

BETTER TELESCOPES

Scientists' ability to study celestial objects and their motions improved tremendously during Johannes Kepler's lifetime, thanks in part to him. The primary tool of modern astronomers is the telescope. Until the early seventeenth century, practical, effective telescopes did not exist. The first ones were invented not by scientists but by spectacle (eyeglass) makers.

Most historians credit Hans Lippershey (1570–1619), a German spectacle maker, with developing the first telescope design in 1608. Claims to the telescope's invention also were made by two Dutch optical instrument makers who worked during the same time, Jacob Metius and Zacharias Janssen. Their designs called for two lenses. The outer lens, which would gather light from distant objects, was convex, bubbled slightly outward in shape. The eyepiece lens at the other end was concave, curved slightly inward at the center. (A round ball is convex; the inside of a coffee cup is concave.) These early designs were termed refractive telescopes because the lenses refracted, or altered, the path of incoming light.

Based on the design patents of these craftsmen, Galileo Galilei actually constructed the first telescope the following year. He fitted concave and convex glass lenses to either end of a lead cylinder. In coming years, he improved his invention. His first telescope magnified objects by a factor of three. In time, he devised a telescope that could amplify distant targets by thirty-three diameters.

Galileo's telescopes were far from perfect. Their enlarged images were fuzzy. Nonetheless, he was able to make important discoveries. He could study the craters and mountains of the moon. He observed the phases of Venus and noted new moons in orbit around Jupiter.

Kepler was very excited by the invention. Galileo was giving telescopes to prominent people to see the potential for themselves. Kepler hoped he would receive one. He did not, but he managed to borrow one from the duke of Bavaria. Kepler wondered what would result if both lenses were convex. He elaborated on this idea in a

The mayor of Danzig, Poland, proudly demonstrates to onlookers his Keplerian telescope, which used convex lenses. This demonstration occurred in 1670, forty years after the astronomer's death.

small book, *Dioptrice* (Dioptics, also known as Refraction), published in 1611. What he suggested came to be known as the Keplerian telescope.

The first Keplerian telescope was not actually constructed until 1630, the year of his death. His innovation, however, marked a great improvement in the viewing of distant objects. It made possible greater magnification and wider fields of view.

By the end of the century, astronomers were equipped with telescopes that were far more useful than those available to Galileo or Kepler. In 1668, Sir Isaac Newton designed the first reflective telescope. Employing mirrors inside the tube, reflective telescopes could be made larger and could receive more light from dimly lit distant objects.

The importance of the telescope cannot be overstated. Modern telescopes are thousands of times more powerful and much more versatile than those of the seventeenth century. Kepler's suggestion for the two lenses represented a significant early advance in telescopic engineering.

NEW HOME, NEW BOOKS

Kepler's book *Dioptrice* is considered a pioneering work on the subject of geometrical optics, a study of the characteristics of light rays and telescope lenses. It's interesting that although it was a valuable endorsement for Galileo of *Sidereus Nuncius,* Galileo showed no gratitude. In the coming years, he ignored Kepler's letters.

Kepler's time in Prague, meanwhile, was coming to a close. In 1611, most of the European continent was on edge with religious and political strife. In some instances, power struggles involved plots within royal families. Emperor Rudolf in Prague ultimately gave up control of Bohemia to his brother Matthias. The city was in turmoil, with fighting between supporters of the royal factions and looting in the streets. Kepler remained loyal to his benefactor but began a frantic search for a new position.

At first, he hoped to receive an appointment at a university in his home duchy, Württemberg. The leaders there rejected him, however, because of his nonconformist religious views. So instead, he accepted a post teaching at a school in Linz, a port city on the Danube River in Oberösterreich (Upper Austria).

Emperor Rudolf, his longtime patron, died in January 1612. Happily, Rudolf's successor, Matthias, let Kepler keep his title as imperial mathematician. But he was not allowed to remain at the royal court in Prague. He took up his post in Linz as what amounted to a provincial mathematician.

While in Upper Austria, Kepler wrote new books that contributed significantly to the study of

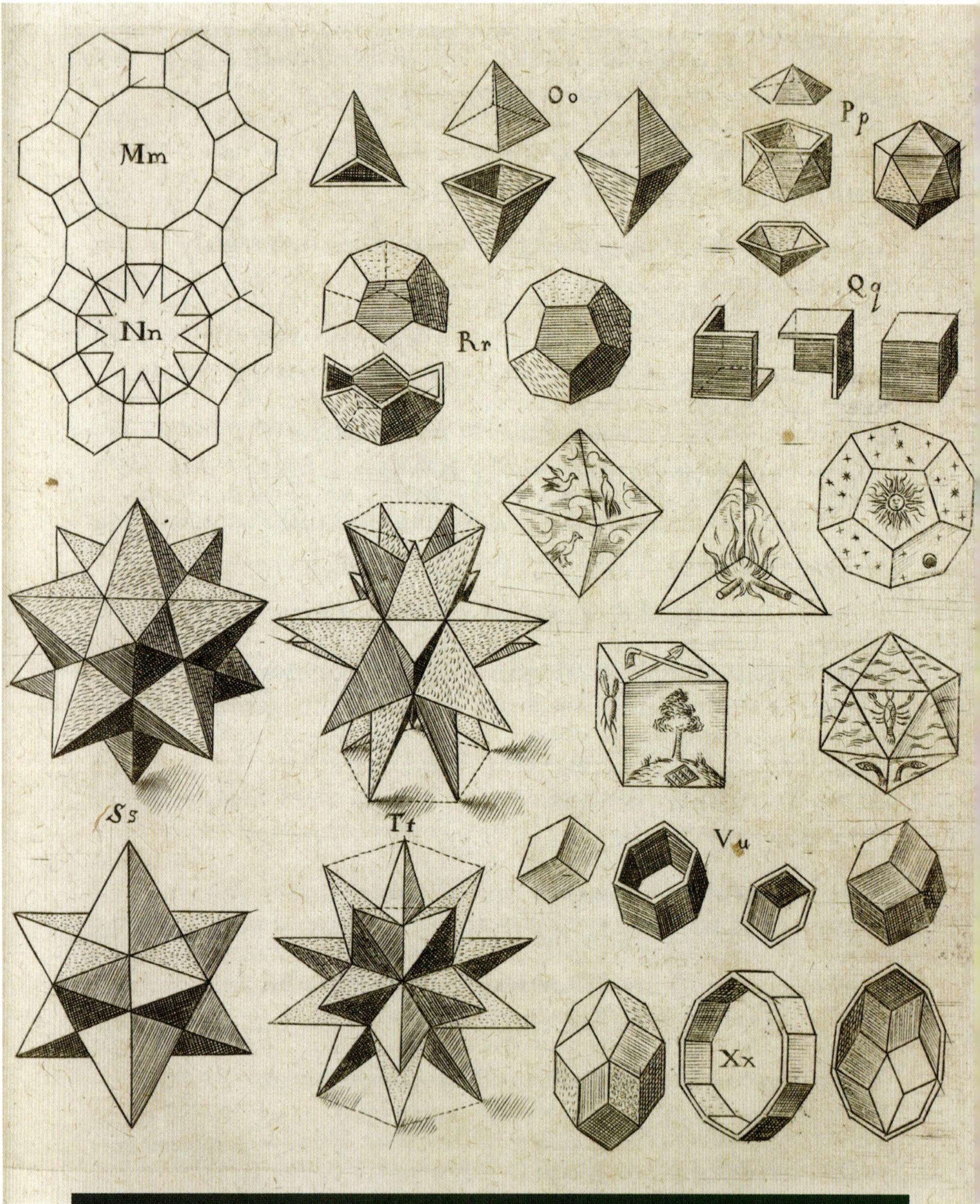

This engraving of geometrical shapes was published in Kepler's *Harmonice Mundi*. The book contained his third planetary law, proposing a mathematical formula to calculate planets' movements and distances.

outer space. *Harmonice Mundi* (*Harmonies of the World*) was published in 1619. It involved principles and ideas related to astronomy, geometry, physics, astrology, and—surprisingly—music. Geometrical harmonies, he believed, pertained not just to musical notation but to the arrangement of the planets.

In *Harmonice Mundi,* Kepler presented his third law concerning the movements of the planets. Essentially, it produced an important mathematical formula. The square of the time it takes a planet to orbit the sun, Kepler found, exactly relates to the cube of the planet's distance from the sun. Using this formula, astronomers could calculate planetary distances by the objects' movements.

Epitome Astronomiae Copernicanae (*Epitome of Copernican Astronomy*) appeared in three volumes from 1618 to 1621. While affirming Copernicus's heliocentric theory, it elaborated on Kepler's own laws of planetary motion.

In Kepler's time, scientists did not regard as "laws" the important findings made by Kepler, Copernicus, and others. To Kepler, they were celestial "harmonies." They were explanations of how God had assembled the universe.

While his writing continued at a prolific pace, Kepler's time at Linz was marred by uncertainty. Religious tension across Europe flamed into open, widespread violence in 1618. It would continue almost unabated for thirty years.

THIRTY YEARS OF WAR

The Thirty Years' War (1618–1648) literally was thirty years of almost continual conflict across Europe. It resulted mainly from decades of deepening tension between Roman Catholics and Protestants during the Protestant Reformation. The situation was complicated by political power struggles. Some of the European emperors and princes in different countries were willing to resort to conflict in their opposition to the Holy Roman emperor.

The war began after Catholic bishops ordered the destruction of Protestant churches in Germany and Bohemia. Protestants in Bohemia appealed to the Holy Roman emperor and to the king of Bohemia to stop the persecution. Their demands were ignored. A furious mob swarmed the palace in Prague and flung two of the king's ministers out of a window.

The rebellion spread to other parts of Europe. A sequence of battles was fought, mainly in Germany, Denmark, Sweden, and France. While religious hostility remained an underlying theme, the war became a complex jockeying for political control of territory. The war finally ended with the Peace of Westphalia, signed in 1648.

Entire towns were obliterated in the course of the fighting. Territorial boundaries were redrawn. The Netherlands and Switzerland became independent states. Historians surmise that Europe—especially Germany—was still coping with the effects of the devastation almost two centuries later.

Although he was destined to become a scientist rather than a clergyman, Kepler never wavered from his deeply religious convictions. This steadfastness was in spite of the Lutheran Church turning against him because of his tolerance for Calvinism. He was refused the privilege of taking Holy Communion in Linz.

He considered his astronomical investigations and theology closely linked. Kepler was convinced God laid out the cosmos in an immensely complex but wonderfully logical design. The providential plan could be understood, he believed, by close scrutiny and analysis.

Nicolaus Copernicus is perhaps better known than Johannes Kepler as a pioneering astronomer during the Scientific Revolution. Kepler, though, contributed greatly to Copernicus's legacy. He established mathematical proof of Copernicus's theory.

CHAPTER SIX

A Family in Turmoil

Living conditions in the time of Johannes Kepler were profoundly different from what they are today. A sketch of Kepler's life would be incomplete without an overview of European life during the upheavals of the period. Their surrounding conditions impacted his family during his childhood and in later years. For Kepler, these issues were complicated by a sobering assortment of personal problems he had to address within his family.

Compared to today's highly advanced medicines and medical procedures, treatments of diseases and physical ailments were grossly primitive. Lifespans were shorter. The customary remedy for a toothache (brutal extraction) could result in mortal complications. Plagues were devastating, wiping out whole populations, because there were no effective treatments. The only survivors were those who miraculously did not contract the disease or were hardy enough to endure it.

Social conditions were appalling by modern standards. People who were physically or mentally challenged rarely received helpful care; they were doomed to short, miserable lives. Religious prejudice often led to violence. Not infrequently, citizens of a town were forced to profess the prevailing doctrine or be cast out. This policy of exclusion affected academics. Teachers who found themselves in situations where their religious beliefs came under fire could lose their livelihoods. Kepler experienced this firsthand.

Criminal punishment typically was severe. Wrongdoings that are considered minor or even pardonable today—stealing food to feed a starving family, for

This scene depicts captives inside a seventeenth-century prison. Incarceration in cold, rodent-infested jails was brutal; many inmates died of starvation or disease.

example—might bring a long term of imprisonment. Subsistence in a dank, dark, rat-infested dungeon with little food and water was a sentence worse than death for countless prisoners. Many died in chains. Outside, some forms of physical punishment were heinously torturous.

Members of Kepler's family languished through many such tribulations. Especially hard were the ordeals of his younger brother Heinrich and, most grimly, his mother.

SIBLING TRAGEDIES

The troubles created by his father were the beginning of a long sequence of woes to afflict the family. Three of Kepler's six younger siblings died in childhood. A sister, Gretchen, married a vicar and apparently lived a relatively ordinary life. Their brother Christopher grew to become a skilled metalworker, specializing in crafting bowls, cups, and other objects of pewter. Apart from them, however, sibling woes abounded.

Their brother Heinrich was an epileptic. Of all the surviving children, Heinrich experienced the most traumatic upbringing. This treatment no doubt resulted in part because of his medical condition. He also suffered from a combination of mishaps, abuses, and mischief. He almost drowned. More than once, he received serious animal bites. He was robbed and beaten and often was sick. He survived the extremes of heat—once almost freezing to death, once almost perishing in a fire. Entering his teens, he became an apprentice to a cloth maker, then to a baker. He failed at both trades.

The father of the family, concluding that young Heinrich was a problem child, determined to sell him. In those times, children were sometimes sold into servitude. The parent received money for his child's labors. But the son revolted. The elder Heinrich's scheme was foiled when the son ran away from home. He led the life of a vagabond, historians believe. He may have earned coins as a beggar, baker, street musician, and drummer with an army corps.

Brother Heinrich's ultimate fate is unclear. By one account, he found his way home and lived with his mother, dying of an unknown cause while only in his early forties. By another, he showed up some years later in Prague to join his older brother Johannes. There, Heinrich reportedly became a soldier in the imperial guard.

KEPLER'S MOTHER—A WITCH?

By far, the most gut-wrenching ordeal of Kepler's life was the accusation that his mother, Katharina, was a witch. Kepler went to her defense, but not all of his siblings agreed. At least one supported her prosecution.

Their mother was not an educated woman. However, she was naturally curious—a trait obviously passed on to Johannes from her, rather than from his wayward father. She collected and experimented with a variety of local herbs, and she mixed healing potions. This practice in time would be presented as evidence in her trial for a mortally serious crime: witchcraft.

Katharina first was accused of witchery in 1615 in Leonberg. She faced forty-nine separate charges. If found guilty, she would be tortured with needles, hot irons, and the rack—a cruel contraption that wrenched limbs from their sockets. In the end she would be burned alive at the stake.

Odds of acquittal were not in her favor. Her memory was not good, hampering her defense. Accused witches were being convicted by the dozen. In Weil der Stadt, Johannes Kepler's hometown, almost forty "witches" were condemned to die at the stake between 1615 and 1630.

The accusations of witchery against Katharina were not really surprising. She sincerely believed in the medicinal—or magical—powers of the potions she concocted. Katharina had been raised by an aunt who had been found guilty of witchcraft and had been burned at the stake.

The evidence against Katharina was unusual. It began with a spark of suspicion. Another woman living in Leonberg claimed Katharina had given her a medicinal potion, which, instead of curing her ailment, had caused a prolonged illness. Others of the town said they

A period woodcut illustrates different devices for torture—often used on accused individuals not yet found guilty. Fire was a popular device applied to induce suspects to "confess."

fell ill after accepting drinks from Katharina. Some said a man who drank the liquid had become paralyzed—and a woman had died.

Others came forth to claim Katharina had cast an "evil eye" on children. A twelve-year-old girl carrying bricks declared she met Katharina Kepler on a road and felt a sudden pain in her arm at that instant, becoming paralyzed. It also was alleged that she could pass through locked doors.

Proceedings against Katharina were drawn out for six years. Her son Heinrich at one point testified that he believed his mother was insane. He reported that she once rode a calf to death to butcher and cook it for a feast.

Throughout the years of proceedings, the trial of his mother held the Kepler family, especially Johannes, in a state of emotional strangulation. Johannes stood in her defense. As imperial mathematician to the Holy Roman emperor, his influence should have been adequate to win her acquittal. However, he was on record disagreeing with certain ironclad principles of the Lutheran Church. This difference of opinion was deemed heresy by church leaders. If he was a heretic, it seemed probable to them that his mother was a witch.

In the end, after stubbornly denying her guilt despite extreme tactics to make her confess, Katharina was found not guilty in September 1621. She was a broken woman, though, and died shortly afterward.

WITCH TRIALS

When Katharina Kepler, Johannes's mother, was tried for witchcraft, she had a lot of company. Women who came to the attention of authorities for being out of the ordinary—who dabbled in herbal potions and offered miraculous cures, for example, or who cast curses or spoke unintelligibly—were considered suspicious. Not only accused witches themselves were at peril. So were their children and various people with whom they were associated. Town mayors and even noblemen were among the defendants linked to witchcraft during the years of the Scientific Revolution. It has been estimated that roughly fifty thousand people were executed for witchcraft and related charges in Europe during the sixteenth and seventeenth centuries.

In many cases, there was no actual evidence against women accused of witchcraft, only rumors. Authorities came up with interesting tests to "prove" a defendant's guilt or innocence. One was to bind the woman with cords and throw her into a pond or river. If she floated—ironically—she was judged to be a witch and was executed. If she sank, she was ruled innocent (and hopefully was pulled from the depths before she drowned).

If found guilty, punishment was rarely light. The convict might be flogged, imprisoned for years, or

(*CONTINUED ON THE NEXT PAGE*)

(CONTINUED FROM THE PREVIOUS PAGE)

exiled from the township or district. A heavy fine might be imposed, if the person's family was wealthy and authorities saw that a profit could be realized for the local government. Death often was the sentence. Some convicted of witchcraft were hanged or beheaded. The most excruciating method of execution was burning alive at the stake.

UNRELENTING GRIEF

His turbulent family life throughout his childhood and the chilling accusations against his mother in later years were not the only afflictions that beset Kepler during his lifetime. A growing vexation was his fourteen-year marriage to his first wife, Barbara. They both became increasingly unhappy.

Barbara showed no interest in his scientific pursuits. Having come from a fairly wealthy family, she was frustrated by her husband's modest salary—which often was paid late. He described her as touchy, nagging, and unloving. She also was prone to sickness and a failing memory, possibly related to her own state of unhappiness with the marriage. Barbara was only thirty-seven when she died in 1611.

After Barbara's death, Kepler did not wait long to seek a new wife to establish a household and take care of his children. In an amusing letter he wrote to a friend in October 1613, he described no fewer than eleven women he had been considering, with his assessment of each as a prospective wife. He decided on Susanna Reuttinger of Efferding. By all accounts, she was much more compatible as a spouse than Barbara, and his second marriage was much happier than his first. Susanna was educated but was not well-to-do. In his letter, Kepler said the traits that won his heart were her "love, humble loyalty, economy of household, diligence, and the love she gave the stepchildren." He added, "Frame, habits, and body conform with mine."

More sorrow was in store, however. Three of their children died within a six-month period between 1617 and 1618.

Artist Vaclav Hollar drew this view of the river port of Linz in 1636. While Kepler's family lived there, the walled city came under siege during the religious wars.

Psychiatrists today almost certainly would diagnose Kepler's life as one of perpetual stress. The many contributors included his frail health, abusive and negligent parentage, abrupt changes in career plans, prolonged conflicts with Tycho Brahe's heirs, unhappy wedlock, and children's deaths—not to mention the religious and political unrest that afflicted all of European society. Kepler faced criticism not only from Catholics but from Protestant leaders. He formally was excommunicated from the Lutheran Church in 1619 because of his unorthodox views.

Clinical depression, as it is classified today, was not understood in those centuries, but it seems likely Kepler endured decades of it. In spite of it all, he was able to make astonishing contributions to science.

CHAPTER SEVEN

Kepler's Last Years

While at Linz, Kepler negotiated a contract to complete Brahe's exhaustive set of planet and star tables, *Tabulae Rudolphinae*. Finally published in 1627 after decades of meticulous research begun by Brahe and finished by Kepler, it was to be his last major work.

By that time, the tribulations of the Reformation and Counter-Reformation had caught up with him again. Ferdinand II, who had become Holy Roman emperor in 1619, had banned all religions except Catholicism in Bohemia. At Prague, more than two dozen Protestant leaders were put to death. The authorities symbolically cut out the tongue of one Lutheran professor, a friend of Kepler's, as a warning against teaching Protestantism.

Executions did not occur in Linz, but some of the Lutheran leaders there were imprisoned.

Kepler at first was exempt from persecution because of his title as imperial mathematician. Also in his favor was his unorthodox religious stance—which had placed him at odds with Protestant leaders. Ferdinand let him remain.

UNDER SIEGE

His situation began to darken in early 1626. All Protestants in Linz were ordered to convert to Catholicism by Easter of that year or be driven from the country. Again, Kepler was granted an exception. Events beyond the emperor's control, however, were turning the crisis into a catastrophe. Protestants in some parts of Upper Austria were harassing Catholic priests. In punishment,

TABULÆ

RUDOLPHINÆ,

QUIBUS ASTRONOMICÆ SCIENTIÆ, TEMPOrum longinquitate collapsæ RESTAURATIO continetur;

A Phœnice illo Astronomorum

TYCHONE,

Ex Illustri & Generosa BRAHEORUM in Regno Daniæ familiâ oriundo Equite,

PRIMUM ANIMO CONCEPTA ET DESTINATA ANNO CHRISTI MDLXIV: EXINDE OBSERVATIONIBUS SIDERUM ACCURATISSIMIS, POST ANNUM PRÆCIPUE MDLXXII, QUO SIDUS IN CASSIOPEIÆ CONSTELLATIONE NOVUM EFFULSIT, SERIÒ AFFECTATA; VARIISQUE operibus, cùm mechanicis, tùm librariis, impenso patrimonio amplissimo, accedentibus etiam subsidiis FRIDERICI II. DANIÆ REGIS, regali magnificentiâ dignis, tracta per annos XXV. potissimùm in Insula freti SUNDICI HUENNA, & arce URANIBURGO, in hos usus à fundamentis extructâ:

TANDEM TRADUCTA IN GERMANIAM, INQUE AULAM ET Nomen RUDOLPHI IMP. anno MDIIC.

TABULAS IPSAS, JAM ET NUNCUPATAS, ET AFFECTAS, SED MORTE AUTHORIS SUI ANNO MDCI. DESERTAS,

JUSSU ET STIPENDIIS FRETUS TRIUM IMPPP.

RUDOLPHI, MATTHIÆ, FERDINANDI,

ANNITENTIBUS HÆREDIBUS BRAHEANIS; EX FUNDAMENTIS OBservationum relictarum; ad exemplum ferè partium jam exstructarum; continuis multorum annorum speculationibus, & computationibus, primùm PRAGÆ Bohemorum continuavit; deinde LINCII, Superioris Austriæ Metropoli, subsidiis etiam Ill. Provincialium adjutus, perfecit, absolvit; adq; causarum & calculi perennis formulam traduxit.

IOANNES KEPLERUS,

TYCHONI primùm à RUDOLPHO II. Imp. adjunctus calculi minister; indéq; Trium ordine Imppp. Mathematicus:

Qui idem de speciali mandato FERDINANDI II. IMP. petentibus instantibúsq; Hæredibus,

Opus hoc ad usus præsentium & posteritatis, typis, numericis propriis, cæteris, & prælo JONÆ SAURII, Reip. Ulmanæ Typographi, in publicum extulit, & Typographicis operis ULMÆ curator affuit.

Cum Privilegiis, IMP. & Regum Rerúmq; publ. vivo TYCHONI ejúsq; Hæredibus, & speciali Imperatorio, ipsi KEPLERO concesso, ad Annos XXX.

ANNO M. DC. XXVII.

These opening pages are from an early edition of the *Tabulae Rudolphinae,* Kepler's final major work on which he had labored for a quarter of a century.

seventeen Protestants were executed. This situation provoked a massive peasant revolt. The rebel horde laid siege to Linz in June. Although the uprising generally was an assault on the Catholic authorities, Kepler and other Protestants in Linz were afraid for their lives. The ungovernable peasants, if they entered and looted the city, could be trusted to spare no one.

Thankfully, Linz was a walled city. Regrettably, the lodgings where Kepler and his family stayed were built into the wall. Throughout the siege, soldiers were constantly inside the apartment. Kepler could get little work done.

The peasants withdrew in August, and Kepler's family members were free to leave. They packed their belongings aboard a boat on the Danube River and relocated to Regensburg, a Protestant-controlled river port 125 miles (200 km) to the northwest, in Germany.

GETTING *TABULAE RUDOLPHINAE* TO PRESS

While his family settled in Regensburg, Kepler went overland to Ulm, where he had arranged for the materials of *Tabulae Rudolphinae*—more than five hundred pages—to be printed. He oversaw every stage of the printing to ensure no errors were made while setting the minutely detailed data in type.

The process took nine months. Printing was completed just in time for Kepler to present copies at the bustling book fair in Frankfurt in September 1627.

Tabulae Rudophinae had been a work in progress for more than a quarter of a century. It was begun by Brahe, whose son-in-law later had been involved. But it was Kepler who brought it to fruition. It had almost entirely consumed his work during the 1620s. Emperor Ferdinand had been impatient to have it finally published, counting on it to generate income for the imperial treasury. Now that the project was finished, Kepler worried that the emperor no longer would want his services.

A sixteenth-century print shows a view of Regensburg (also called Ratispon), a Protestant port city where Kepler ultimately moved his family. He died there in 1630.

He had logical reasons to fear. Ferdinand had purged all Protestants from his court. When Kepler went to Prague in December 1627 to formally present Ferdinand with a copy of *Tabulae Rudolphinae*, he was the only Protestant there. Surprisingly, Ferdinand—well pleased with the book—assured him that his title as imperial mathematician was secure … on one condition. Kepler must renounce his Lutheran faith and become a Roman Catholic. Kepler bravely refused, casting his future in bleak uncertainty.

His dilemma came to an unexpectedly pleasant resolution. Albrecht Wenzel Eusebius von Wallenstein, a wealthy imperial general, intervened to become his patron. Wallenstein, who had converted to Catholicism but was tolerant to Protestants, firmly believed in the prophesies of astrologers. He particularly respected the horoscopes prepared by Kepler.

Kepler agreed to provide Wallenstein with astrological calculations. (The horoscopes he devised turned out to contain at least one chilling accuracy—the suggestion of Wallenstein's murder in 1634.) Wallenstein set Kepler up in Sagan, a city in Silesia (now in Poland). Almost as important to Kepler as Wallenstein's financial aid was the building of a printing press for his personal use. Kepler and his family settled in Sagan in the summer of 1628.

But Kepler was not to enjoy a well-deserved respite in his declining years. Sagan at the time was predominantly

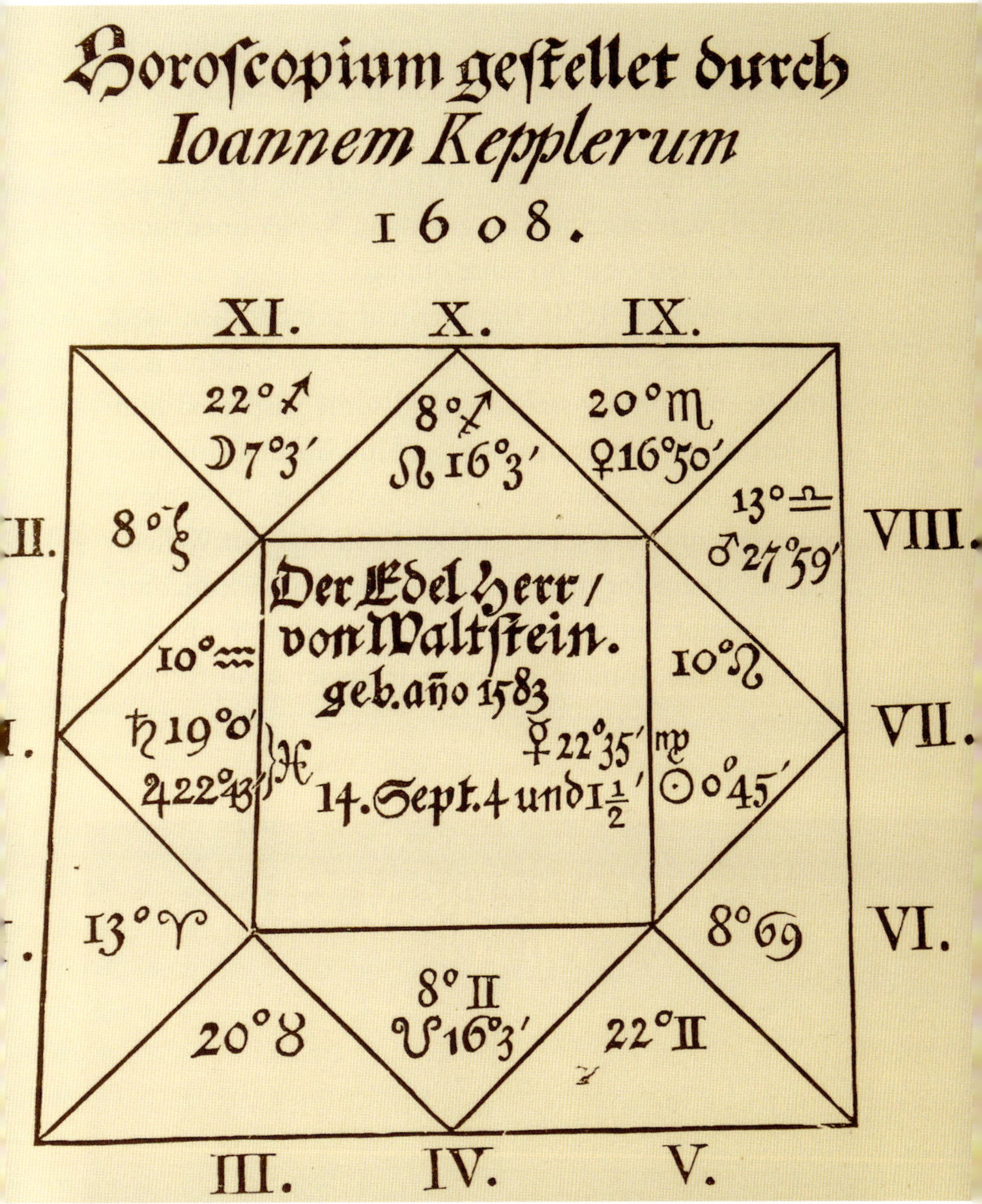

This is one of the horoscopes that Kepler is believed to have prepared for Albrecht Wenzel Eusebius von Wallenstein, his benefactor, shortly before Kepler died.

Protestant, but Ferdinand's determination to Catholicize his entire kingdom soon overtook the city. Books written by Protestants were banned. Residents were given the familiar ultimatum: convert to the Catholic faith or get out. With Wallenstein as his guardian, Kepler once more received amnesty, but no sense of peace.

In August 1630, the German princes dismissed Wallenstein as imperial general. They were displeased with recent military setbacks, and some suspected him of plotting to take control of the Holy Roman Empire. The loss of his patronage was the final blow in Kepler's long series of stresses. He had been counting on Wallenstein to obtain for him a small fortune in back income that Emperor Ferdinand had failed to pay over a period of years. This hope of receiving financial security now was lost.

A "DREAM" FROM THE GRAVE

When Kepler was a seminary student at Tübingen in the 1590s, he wrote a strange essay. If he lived on the moon, he wondered, how would the solar system appear from that vantage point? He added notes to it over the years. By the end of his life, *Somnium* (*The*

Dream) had been expanded to the length of a short book, although he had not quite completed it.

Characters and events in *Somnium* in part reflected Kepler's life. The hero was a young man whose mother—like his own—dabbled with herbs and mysticism. She conjured up a demon that transported her son to the moon.

Kepler's description of life on the moon (which is nonexistent) was fascinating, if unrealistic. He described serpentine monsters, mountains higher than those on Earth, and circular walled cities (which would appear to earthlings as lunar craters). Residents of the moon, he wrote, had to endure horrific weather extremes: ice storms driven by ferocious winds at night, scorching days fifteen times hotter than in the African deserts.

The focus of the work was astronomy. Kepler depicted the planets, sun, and other celestial objects in bizarre motions through the solar system. This weird pattern of sightings resulted from the moon's revolutions around Earth.

Somnium was not published until 1634, four years after Kepler's death. Some historians and literary scholars consider it the first work of modern science fiction. Biographer Arthur Koestler termed it Kepler's "lunar nightmare."

EPITAPH FOR AN IMPORTANT ASTRONOMER

Johannes Kepler died on November 15, 1630, at Regensburg. He had gone there to try to collect some of the money that was owed to him through investments he had made. Immediately upon arriving, he came down with a fever and could not overcome it. He never had been physically strong. Perhaps the severe trials of the last few years had robbed him of the will to continue. According to Koestler, one year before his death, Kepler had made a statement in a letter that seems eerily prophetic: "When the storm rages and the state is threatened by shipwreck, we can do nothing more noble than to lower the anchor of our peaceful studies into the ground of eternity."

To the very end, he kept his Lutheran faith. When asked on his deathbed if he expected eternal life and salvation, Kepler weakly asserted that he trusted, as stated by historian James A. Connor, "solely in Christ, from whom comes all solace, welfare, and protection."

The graveyard where Kepler was buried was destroyed during the Thirty Years' War, and no grave marker exists. However, according to *Ptolemy, Copernicus, Kepler*, edited by Robert Maynard Hutchins, not long before his death, Kepler wrote down his own epitaph in poetic form:

I had measured the heavens;
Now I measure earth's shadows.
Mind came from the heavens,
Body's shadow has fallen.

KEPLER GOES INTO ORBIT

On March 7, 2009, the US National Aeronautics and Space Administration (NASA) launched an ambitious new mission from Cape Canaveral, Florida. It was a small, unmanned observatory, which would follow Earth in its orbit around the sun. Its purpose: to examine a section of the Milky Way in search of Earth-like planets that might be circling distant sun/stars. Such planets are called extrasolar planets, or exoplanets. The name of the observatory: *Kepler*. It had been in development for several decades.

The observatory was fitted with a powerful photometer, an instrument that measures the intensity of a source of light. *Kepler*'s task was to monitor the radiations of some 145,000 stars. A slight dimming of intensity would suggest that a planet was passing across the line of vision in its orbit around the star.

The mission was an immediate success. Within six months after the spacecraft began transmitting data

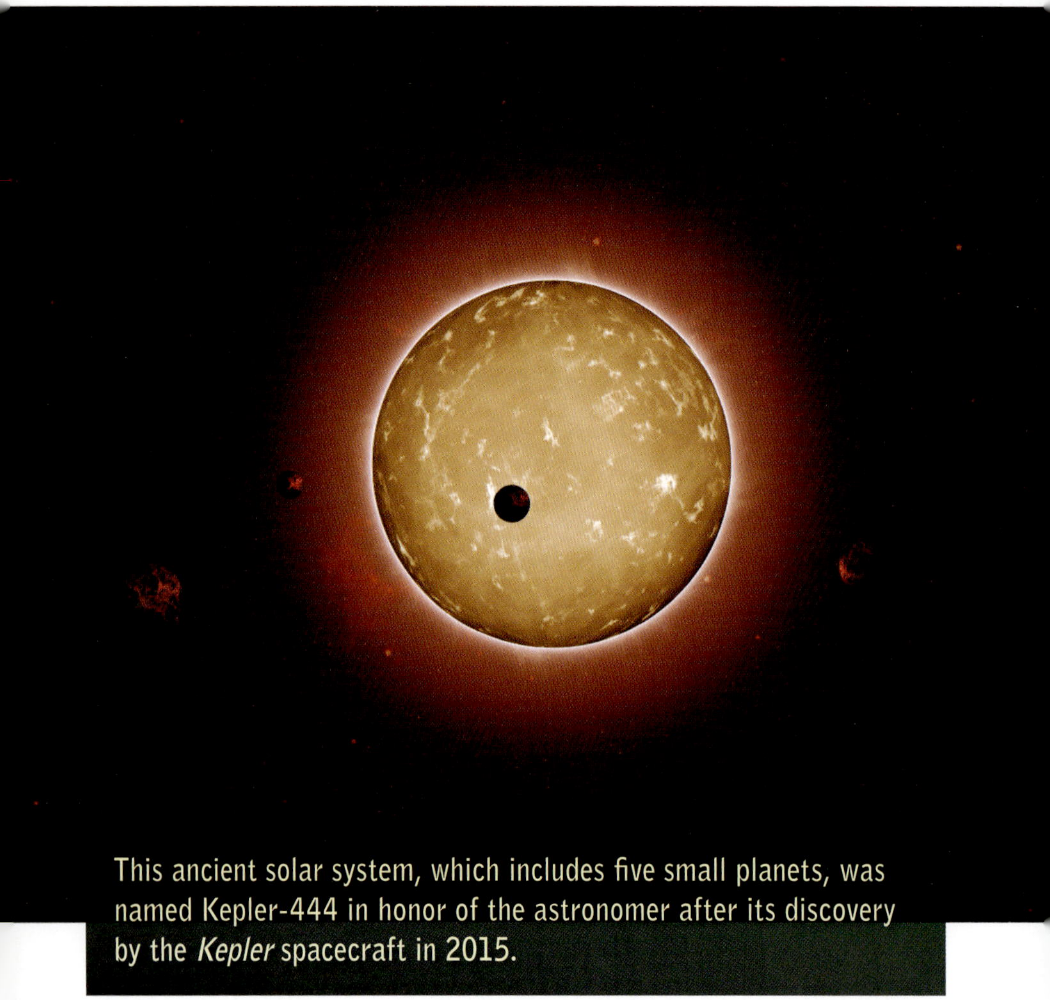

This ancient solar system, which includes five small planets, was named Kepler-444 in honor of the astronomer after its discovery by the *Kepler* spacecraft in 2015.

back to Earth, it had monitored almost one thousand stars and found more than fifty potential Earth-size exoplanets. Theoretically, exoplanets of this type could be orbiting their suns within habitable zones.

In November 2012, NASA announced that *Kepler*'s stated mission had been completed—but it was not over. NASA decided to continue operating the telescope for another four years. As of December 2016, *Kepler* had identified more than 2,300 confirmed exoplanets and detected almost 5,000 possible exoplanets.

KEPLER'S LEGACY

The name of Johannes Kepler may not be as familiar to the masses as those of Copernicus, Galileo, and Newton. Nonetheless, his findings were vitally important to all later astronomers' understanding of the solar system. In the generation following his death in 1630, many astronomers embraced the school of scientific thought dubbed "Keplerian Copernicanism."

Like many great people in history, Johannes Kepler was a man of contradictions. He possessed weaknesses as well as strengths. What may be most remarkable about him is that his lifelong physical weakness—his eyesight—did not prevent his pioneering research and observations during the Scientific Revolution. Biographer Koestler observed, "The myopic child, who sometimes saw the world doubled or quadrupled, became the founder of modern optics … the man who could see clearly only at a short distance invented the modern astronomical telescope."

Timeline

1571 Johannes Kepler is born on December 27 in Weil der Stadt, Germany.

1577–1589 Kepler attends German and Latin secondary schools.

1588 Kepler's father abandons the family and is not heard from again.

1589 Kepler begins theological studies at the University of Tübingen.

1594 Studies to enter the clergy end when Kepler accepts a mathematics teaching post in Graz, Austria.

1596 *Mysterium Cosmographicum*, Kepler's first book, is published.

1597 Barbara Mühleck and Kepler are married in Graz.

1600 Tycho Brahe, imperial mathematician, invites Kepler to work with him in Prague, Bohemia.

1601 Kepler becomes Emperor Rudolf II's mathematician when Brahe dies.

1604 *Astronomiae Pars Optica* is published.

1609 *Astronomia Nova* is published.

1612 Kepler becomes a mathematics teacher in Linz, Austria.

1613 Susanna Reuttinger and Kepler are married two years after the death of his first wife.

1615–1621 Witchcraft trial of Kepler's mother takes place.

1618–1621 *Epitome Astronomiae Copernicanae* is published in three volumes.

1619 *Harmonice Mundi* is published.

1627 *Tabulae Rudolphinae* is published.

1628 Kepler relocates to Sagan, Silesia.

1630 Kepler dies in Regensburg, Germany, on November 15.

GLOSSARY

ASTROLOGY The study of how the sun and stars and the motions of the planets and moon seem to affect events on Earth.

CELESTIAL Referring to the heavenly bodies.

COMPOSITE A material formed by combining two or more substances.

COSMOLOGIST Scientist who studies the universe.

COSMOS The universe as an orderly, harmonious system.

DIALECTICS Verbalizing logical thoughts.

DOCTRINE A line of beliefs and principles.

DUCHY Domain controlled by a duke.

ELLIPSES Oval shapes.

EPILEPTIC Person who suffers from a medical disorder characterized by convulsions and loss of consciousness.

GENEALOGICAL Relating to a person's ancestry.

HEINOUS Evil or wicked.

HERESY A belief that is contrary to church teaching.

HOROSCOPE A forecast by an astrologer.

MERCENARY Someone who is hired to serve in a foreign army.

MYSTICISM A belief that truths and prophesies can be derived through intuition and the senses.

NONCONFORMIST One who does not agree with majority views concerning religion, politics, education, etc.

ORBIT Path traced by an object in its regular revolution around another object.

PEWTER An alloy that typically combines tin or lead with another metal.

RHETORIC Skillful speech or writing.

SACRILEGIOUS Profane or unholy.

THEOLOGICAL Relating to religion.

VICAR Member of the clergy of certain Protestant denominations.

For More Information

American Astronomical Society (AAS)
1667 K Street NW, Suite 800
Washington, DC 20006
(202) 328-2010
Website: https://aas.org
The AAS promotes astronomical studies and related branches of science. It also supports educational programs in astronomy.

The Astronomical League
9201 Ward Parkway, Suite 100
Kansas City, MO 64114
(816) 333-7759
Website: http://www.astroleague.org
The organization fosters astronomical education. It is an umbrella league composed of some 240 amateur astronomy societies.

National Aeronautics and Space Administration (NASA)
300 E Street SW, Suite 5R30
Washington, DC 20546
(202) 358-0001
Website: http://www.nasa.gov
NASA maintains a web section devoted to the *Kepler* satellite mission. It includes information about Johannes Kepler's life, work, and discoveries, as well as about the results of the mission.

Royal Astronomical Society
Burlington House

Piccadilly
London W1J 0BQ
United Kingdom
+44 (0)20 7734 4582
+44 (0)20 7734 3307
Website: http://www.ras.org.uk
Founded in 1820, the London organization presents meetings, publishes research, and maintains an extensive library of astronomical material.

Royal Astronomical Society of Canada (RASC)
203-4920 Dundas Street
West Toronto, ON M9A 1B7
Canada
(888) 924-7272
(416) 924-7973
Website: http://www.rasc.ca
The RASC has more than five thousand members including professional astronomers, educators, and amateurs. It sponsors numerous public events and publishes books, calendars, journals, and newsletters.

The Royal Society of Canada
Walter House
282 Somerset West
Ottawa, ON K2P 0J6
Canada
(613) 991-6990
Website: http://www.rsc-src.ca

The primary objective of the society is to promote learning and research in the arts, humanities, and natural and social sciences. It produces newsletters, guides, videos, and other resources.

Smithsonian Institution
PO Box 37012
SI Building, Room 153, MRC 010
Washington, DC 20013-7012
(202) 633-1000
Website: https://www.si.edu
The Smithsonian maintains a wealth of information and resources on all topics, including science. It includes nineteen museums, such as the Natural History Museum and the Air and Space Museum, and galleries as well as the National Zoological Park.

WEBSITES

Because of the changing nature of internet links, Rosen Publishing has developed an online list of websites related to the subject of this book. This site is updated regularly. Please use this link to access the list:

http://www.rosenlinks.com/LOSR/kepler

For Further Reading

Anderson, Michael, ed. *Pioneers in Astronomy and Space Exploration* (Inventors and Innovators). New York, NY: Britannica Educational Publishing, 2013.

Andronik, Catherine M. *Copernicus: Genius of Modern Astronomy* (Genius Scientists and Their Genius Ideas). Berkeley Heights, NJ: Enslow Publishers, 2015.

Bortz, Fred. *Johannes Kepler and the Three Laws of Planetary Motion* (Revolutionary Discoveries of Scientific Pioneers). New York, NY: Rosen Publishing, 2014.

Bortz, Fred. *The Sun-Centered Universe and Nicolaus Copernicus* (Revolutionary Discoveries of Scientific Pioneers). New York, NY: Rosen Publishing, 2014.

Hollar, Sherman, ed. *Astronomy: Understanding the Universe* (The Solar System). New York, NY: Britannica Educational Publishing, 2012.

Jankowski, Connie. *Astronomers: From Copernicus to Crisp* (Mission: Science Collective Biographies). Minneapolis, MN: Compass Point Books, 2008.

Kazlow, Samuel, ed. *Astronomy: Understanding Celestial Bodies* (The Study of Science). New York, NY: Britannica Educational Publishing, 2015.

Kraul, Walter. *Astronomy for Young and Old: A Beginner's Guide to the Visible Sky*. Edinburgh, UK: Floris Books, 2014.

Kruesi, Liz. *Astronomy* (Cutting-Edge Science and Technology). Minneapolis, MN: Essential Library, 2016.

Miller, Ron. *Recentering the Universe: The Radical Theories of Copernicus, Kepler, Galileo, and Newton.* Minneapolis, MN: Twenty-First Century Books, 2014.

Powers, Don, and John B. Beaver. *Astronomy: Our Solar System and Beyond.* Greensboro, NC: Mark Twain Media, 2010.

Rogers, Kara, ed. *The 100 Most Influential Scientists of All Time* (The Britannica Guide to the World's Most Influential People). New York, NY: Britannica Educational Publishing, 2010.

Bibliography

Balchin, Jon. *100 Scientists Who Changed the World* (Science). New York, NY: Enchanted Lion Books, 2003.

Bell, Jim. *The Space Book: From the Beginning to the End of Time, 250 Milestones in the History of Space & Astronomy*. New York, NY: Sterling, 2013.

Caspar, Max. *Kepler* (Life of Science Library). New York, NY: Abelard-Schuman, 1959.

Connor, James A. *Kepler's Witch: An Astronomer's Discovery of Cosmic Order Amid Religious War, Political Intrigue, and the Heresy Trial of His Mother*. San Francisco, CA: HarperSanFrancisco, 2004.

Ferguson, Kitty. *Tycho & Kepler: The Unlikely Partnership That Forever Changed Our Understanding of the Heavens*. New York, NY: Walker & Company, 2002.

Gilder, Joshua, and Anne-Lee Gilder. *Heavenly Intrigue: Johannes Kepler, Tycho Brahe, and the Murder Behind One of History's Greatest Scientific Discoveries*. New York, NY: Doubleday, 2004.

Hutchins, Robert Maynard, ed. *Ptolemy, Copernicus, Kepler* (Great Books of the Western World). Chicago, IL: Encyclopedia Britannica, Inc., 1952.

Koestler, Arthur. *The Watershed: A Biography of Johannes Kepler* (Science Study Series). Garden City, NY: Anchor Books, 1960.

National Aeronautics and Space Administration. "Kepler and K2: Mission Overview." Retrieved October 2016. http://www.nasa.gov/mission_pages/kepler/overview/index.html.

Rundetaarn (Round Tower). "Tycho Brahe." Retrieved September 2016. http://www.rundetaarn.dk/en/the-observatory/tycho-brahe.

Sunshine, Glenn. "Johannes Kepler (1571–1630)." *Christian Worldview Journal*, June 25, 2012. http://www.colsoncenter.org/the-center/columns/indepth/18026-johannes-kepler-1571-1630.

Tierney, John. "Murder! Intrigue! Astronomers?" *New York Times*, November 29, 2010. http://www.nytimes.com/2010/11/30/science/30tierney.html?_r=0.

Voelkel, James R. *Johannes Kepler and the New Astronomy* (Oxford Portraits in Science). New York, NY: Oxford University Press, 1999.

"Weil der Stadt—Keplerstadt." City website. Retrieved September 2016. http://www.weil-der-stadt.de.

INDEX

J

K

L

M

P

R

S

T

W

ABOUT THE AUTHOR

Daniel E. Harmon has written numerous books, mainly for juvenile and young adult readers, on topics ranging from geography to history and health. His works include biographies of Neil Armstrong and early European explorers and navigators. One of his books is *The Early Days of Space Exploration* (From Earth to the Stars series), published by Britannica Educational Publishing. He also contributed to *Science: Its History and Development* (The Study of Science). Harmon, who has also written a multitude of articles, is a longtime magazine and newsletter editor. He lives in Spartanburg, South Carolina.

PHOTO CREDITS:

Cover, p. 1 (portrait) Stock Montage/Archive Photos/Getty Images; cover, p. 1 (background) Hulton Archive/Getty Images; p. 5 Orlicka Galerie, Rychnov nad Kneznou, Czech Republic/Bridgeman Images; p. 9 DEA/G. Dagli Orti/De Agostini/Getty Images; pp. 10–11 Detlev van Ravenswaay/Science Source; pp. 12–13 Universal Images Group/Getty Images; p. 15 Erich Lessing/Art Resource, NY; p. 22 DEA/A. Dagli Orti/De Agostini/Getty Images; p. 24 ZU_09/E+/Getty Images; pp. 26–27, 35 Bettmann/Getty Images; p. 29 De Agostini Picture Library/Getty Images; p. 33 Adina Tovy/Lonely Planet Images/Getty Images; p. 37 Danita Delimont/Gallo Images/Getty Images; pp. 40, 50–51, 61, 70 Science and Society Picture Library/Getty Images; p. 44 ullstein bild/Getty Images; p. 48 Historical Picture Archives/Corbis Historical/Getty Images; p. 55 Heritage Images/Hulton Fine Art Collection/Getty Images; p. 57 NYPL/Science Source/Getty Images; pp. 62–63 Leemage/Universal Images Group/Getty Images; pp. 66–67 Three Lions/Hulton Archive/Getty Images; p. 75 De Agostini/L. Visconti/Getty Images; p. 79 Time Life Pictures/The LIFE Picture Collection/Getty Images; p. 83 Werner Forman/Hulton Fine Art Collection/Getty Images; pp. 86–87, 91 Universal History Archive/Universal Images Group/Getty Images; pp. 88–89 DEA/R. Merlo/De Agostini/Getty Images; p. 96 Tiago Campante/Peter Devine; back cover, pp. 8, 20, 32, 47, 60, 74, 85 agsandrew/Shutterstock.com; pp. 17, 18, 25, 42, 54, 72, 73, 81, 82, 92, 93, 98–111 (background pattern) Ilya Bolotov/Shutterstock.com.

Designer: Brian Garvey; Senior Editor: Kathy Kuhtz Campbell; Photo Researcher: Nicole Baker